THE
LECTOR

THE LECTOR

EFFECTIVE DELIVERY OF THE WORD

Mary Lyons

PASTORAL PRESS
PORTLAND · OREGON

ISBN 156929-035-0

© 2000 Mary Lyons
Pastoral Press
A Division of OCP Publications
5536 N.E. Hassalo
Portland, OR 97213
Phone: 800-LITURGY (548-8749)
Email: liturgy@ocp.org
Web site: www.pastoralpress.com
Web site: www.ocp.org

Library of Congress Cataloging-in-Publication Data

Lyons, Mary, date.
    The lector: effective delivery of the Word / Mary Lyons.
      p. cm.
    ISBN 1-56929-035-0 (pbk.)
     1. Lay readers—Catholic Church. I. Title.

BX1915 .L96 2000
264'.02034—dc21   00-038539

CONTENTS

FOREWORD

The book you are about to read fills a very real void in the pastoral life of the Church. Its clear, practical and often charming tone addresses a need nearly every pastor or lector I know has expressed. Simply put, how does the lay lector appropriately prepare him or herself for this vital public ministry? As every artist knows, fundamentals, technique, skills and polished preparation are but a necessary part of the equation. Where this volume succeeds additionally is in its challenge to the reader to embrace awe, beauty and faith when the Scriptures are proclaimed.

The Fathers of the Second Vatican Council certainly expressed this reverence for the Scriptures in every document they produced. Over and over again, the documents quote Scripture as support and mandate. It was their hope that the Scriptures would illumine every believer, every liturgy, every home and faith community. The calling forth of lay participation in the liturgy, particularly in the area of Scripture, was an expression of the council's rededication to the Bible.

It is, of course, a mistake to believe that Sacred Scripture was not at the heart of Church from its inception. We know that the early Church sang psalms and read the ancient texts of its Jewish tradition. Furthermore, the early believers passed down the stories and teachings of Jesus in an oral tradition which prefigures the proclamation at our liturgies today.

It is true with the codification of liturgical practice throughout the centuries, the responsibility of proclaiming the scripture publicly became the reserve of clerics. But the longest tradition of our Church proclaims that "ignorance of Scripture, is ignorance of Christ" (St. Jerome). Indeed, the Tridentine Mass, the devotions and all the sacraments of the Church were filled with deeply scriptural quotations and prayers. It is sadly amusing to hear some Catholics or other Christians incorrectly claim that Catholics do not have a "scriptural church." The truth is that the teachings of the Church have always searched through and quoted the Bible as the basis for our beliefs and liturgical practices. However, the Fathers of Vatican II rightly recognized that Scripture centeredness needed universal revival.

When Pope Paul VI declared in the *motu proprio Ministeria quaedam* "two ministries, adapted to present-day needs, are to be preserved in the whole Latin Church, namely, those of reader and acolyte," he opened the way for the lay reader. Harkening back to our earliest days, some from the community are called to announce the living presence of Christ through the proclamation of the revealed word.

It is not a ministry for anyone or everyone. It is not a ministry for the unprepared, the unskilled, the inexperienced or the faithless. Yet so often we have witnessed off-handed, incomprehensible or embarrassingly inappropriate persons attempting to read Scripture publicly. Time and again, one hears horror stories of mangled, garbled and irreverent proclamation.

This book recognizes these problems and convincingly leads the reader through the process of becoming an effective lector. Drawing on her faith, her professional background and her commitment to excellent public worship, Mary Lyons has succeeded in producing a work that is both inspiring and real. Do the Church a favor and make sure every pastor, reader or church leader you know gets a copy of this. Remember the warning of Scripture: "How will they believe unless there is someone to announce the Good News?" and announce it well!

The Very Reverend Dennis M. Corrado, C.O.
Provost, Brooklyn Oratory of Saint Philip Neri

PRELUDE

We usually associate May with sun, warmth and flowers — and in our parish, cherry blossoms. It would have been nice if it had been all these things the day I made my First Communion, and again when I was confirmed. Today, May 5th, is a miserable day, dark, with rain pouring mercilessly, tearing apart the delicate blossoms Spring brought us. I remember how it has rained on every important occasion in my life, so it seems appropriate that it is raining as I begin this book.

It is not by chance that I am beginning on May 5th — today is my mother's birthday, and it is for her that this book is being written. Monsignor Robert E. Welsh also played a very important role when he first spoke to me about a program for lectors. It was he who suggested the idea which was the springboard for this book, and my mother, with her gentle spirit, provided the inspiration. Her sharing and joy in all my professional activities and performances were never equaled by her reaction to my being a lector.

The ways of the Lord are often strange and incomprehensible. It was and still is incomprehensible to many people to find me involved in something so totally divorced from music; maybe I was the person most surprised. My musical education and performances began long before school age and have continued throughout my life. Most definitely, the Holy Spirit prompted Monsignor Welsh to suggest that I undertake a training program for lectors in addition to being a lector myself. But the Holy Spirit must have prompted again, prompted me to accept Monsignor's suggestions, thereby opening a whole new vista to me; I was unprepared for the impact it would have on my life.

Being a lector and having the privilege of proclaiming God's word is something that defies description. Whatever I have done in performance, right up to that exalted temple of music, Carnegie Hall, is totally eclipsed by my feelings as a lector. No words can explain what it means to say: "The word of the Lord," and to realize that I have had the awesome responsibility and tremendous opportunity to verbalize God's word, and thereby bring it to life for the congregation. Through Monsignor Welsh's suggestion, I have had this wonderful gift, the ministry of lector.

There was a group of lectors in our parish who were the first I trained more than twenty years ago. They were so willing to learn and cooperate that they made my work a joy and a success. The friendships that ensued, in particular one very special relationship that changed my life, were God's gift to me, and I am forever grateful to all of them, and to him!

Mary Lyons
May 5, 1999

P.S. The sun came out beautifully on May 6th.

PART ONE: THE LECTOR AS A PERSON

**"Let's start at the very beginning,
a very good place to start."**

Most people would expect a book dealing with the proclamation of Scripture to begin with a quote from Isaiah, Revelation or another part of the Bible. No one, probably most of all the Jewish lyricist himself, would ever imagine that a book of this nature would start with a quotation from the pen of Oscar Hammerstein. But, as he wrote in *The Sound of Music,* the "beginning is a very good place to start!"

Lectors do not "happen." Much work and preparation are needed. Granted, some people are endowed with more God-given abilities than others. But regardless of innate talent, much work must be done. I always feel any accomplishment depends on two things: inspiration and perspiration. Inspiration is that which has come from God as a special gift, and perspiration is your reciprocal gift to God in appreciation, as you strive to develop and better your talent.

How many things are taken for granted! We all come into this world with a very precious gift from God, a voice. Some voices are better than others, but nonetheless, everyone has that priceless treasure, which most of us do not fully appreciate. A few days of severe laryngitis, making communication difficult, if not impossible, and we can sense the tremendous value of our ability to speak.

Yet we accept our voices so easily and unappreciatively. Very few of us have studied the anatomy and physiology of the vocal mechanism, or tried to better its use. Even many speech courses fail to spend time on the instrument itself and dwell instead on the composition rather than the delivery of a speech, thus becoming glorified classes in writing.

Becoming a lector is an ideal reason for trying to improve one's voice, one's delivery and, in fact, one's entire approach to using that instrument. The time and effort given to improve yourself for this ministry is never wasted. Not only does it allow for a better understanding and projection of voice, but also for a better understanding of the text, thereby creating a deeper spirituality. Lectoring enriches one's faith and at the same time enhances one's vocal delivery in everyday activities.

Involvement in this ministry does not leave one unchanged. From my own personal experience, as well as observing others whom I have trained, I have noticed the workings of the Holy Spirit, deepening our faith and bringing us closer to God. One cannot be seriously involved in a ministry such as this and remain untouched. I like to think of it as the Lord's reaction to the lector's actions. God is certainly not unappreciative, failing to respond to our efforts; whatever you put into your lectoring will be more than amply repaid.

Appearance and Attitude

Before we discuss "Getting to the church on time" and the lector as a minister, let us stop and address the lector as a person and reflect on some of those things that must be an important part of the preparation — the demeanor and poise appropriate for this ministry.

Many times when I give lectures to lectors (Now there's a tongue-twister for you!), before I begin someone will approach me and ask if I will address the issue of attire. At first this was a surprise to me, because it would seem anyone with a genuine realization of this ministry and all it entails would have the good sense to execute judgment in selecting proper dress. However, the outfits worn to proclaim the word are often disturbing.

Taste and price are not synonymous; something that is expensive and in the latest fashion is not necessarily appropriate to be worn on the altar. The females face the bigger problems, because there are fewer options for men. Often, younger girls wear very short skirts, not realizing the ambo is elevated, making the skirt appear even shorter. We should not even have to discuss necklines because it would seem to me that common sense and dignity for this ministry should dictate what is fitting and acceptable. Sleeveless dresses, particularly those with largely cut armholes, are taboo, as is clothing that is too clingy or ill-fitting.

Most churches have some form of cooling system in the summer months. Hosiery (stockings) will never cause anyone to faint from heat. Feet, even with manicured and painted nails, whether they are in sandals or whatever, are inappropriate without some type of stocking or covering. The thin fabric of these will never cause discomfort but will complete the outfit with suitable modesty.

Accessories are included in attire. Jewelry should not be ostentatious or noisy. Chains or bracelets that are loose and clattery are picked up by the microphone and are disruptive. Always remember — whether it is jewelry, make-up or the outfit, nothing should ever be obvious enough to call attention to itself, rather, everything should be complimentary to the wearer. If you can, look at photographs of Jacqueline Kennedy Onassis or Princess Diana. Though you may not have their budgets, notice how beautifully and modestly they were attired with jewelry in perfect harmony with the outfit and not over-bearing. They dressed simply elegantly and elegantly simple.

If you normally wear make-up, do not arrive at church without it, whether because of inadequate management of preparation time or some misguided sense of piety. If the lector looks unusually pale and wan, the congregation might well be distracted, wondering if the readings will be completed before there is a reenactment of the final scene of *Camille*. Make-up should not call attention to itself. Avoid the "in" shades of lipstick even if they are featured on the cover of *Vogue*. Though they may be popular, some very vibrant reds or shades of deep purple may suggest Halloween. Keep within the normal shades and there should be no problem. Wear what is becoming to your own skin tones and not something that is the latest fad.

We have spent much time discussing the female lectors. Do not think I am being sexist about this. Men have an easier task. A suit is a suit is a suit! Either slacks and a jacket or a suit and a tie is always an acceptable outfit. Never wear jeans, sneakers or any sport attire that suggests a hurried trip from the gym or the ballpark.

Anyone would be excited to receive an invitation to dinner at the White House regardless of one's political affiliations. To dine with the President! How elaborate the preparations would be! Choosing just the right outfit, jewelry to conform, a trip to a hair stylist — everything to look the very best. We would try to be careful about our speech and attempt to rid ourselves of regionalisms — proper diction would be considered a must. We would imagine or mentally rehearse topics of conversation in order to dialogue intelligently and impress our dinner partners with our appreciation and understanding of their fields of endeavor. I could go on about the extent of preparedness for such an occasion.

Yet, we are constantly invited to be a guest at that most special banquet, the Mass, and often, little or no time is spent to be ready for it. Frequently, we do not even adjust our schedules properly to arrive on time. You, as a lector, are indeed a most special guest and have been given the singular honor and privilege of proclaiming his word. Value that honor and spend the necessary time on your appearance and in preparation for the task at hand.

Preparing for Mass

When does your role as a lector begin? Not with "A reading from. . . ." It really starts when you leave home to go to church. It is impossible to arrive only minutes before Mass and do a proper job. No lector should reach the sacristy less than fifteen minutes prior to the scheduled time for Mass. That is a minimum allowance!

In the concert and theater world, we have what is known as a "call," the time when you are contractually obliged to be on the premises. It is always considerably ahead of curtain time. I remember some years ago going to see the veteran thespians Claudette Colbert and Rex Harrison in a Broadway play. We were preparing to park our car prior to having a leisurely dinner when two limousines brought them to the theater. The show had been running several months at this point, yet these two marvelous artists arrived hours ahead, early enough to make the necessary preparations for the performance. It was not a show which required long periods of time spent on make-up; the most important part of the preparation for any performance is the mental aspect —

the time spent in getting into character and focusing on the job at hand. That is what these two artists were allowing for, as would any performers of their caliber.

You cannot dash into the sacristy moments before Mass and expect to do justice to the word, to yourself or to the congregation. Fifteen minutes is indeed short — probably too short. Just to touch on a few items (which will later be discussed more fully) that need attention at that time:

- If the lector is the leader of the General Intercessions (Prayer of the Faithful), in most parishes he will be seeing them for the first time. This includes the names of the sick and deceased.

- The pagination of the lectionary needs to be studied and absorbed so the eyes focus in the proper places. The words are probably arranged differently from the way they were printed in whatever preparation sources were used. Also, check to make certain the ribbon marker is in the correct page.

- Remember to adjust the microphone to suit your height, and make certain it is turned on. Never, ever knock on it to ascertain whether it is working. Treat it kindly and the microphone will respond in like manner by nicely amplifying your voice.

Demeanor throughout Mass

Probably everyone has had the experience of going on an interview, or in my own profession, an audition. If you were well trained and counseled in the art of being interviewed or auditioned, you were made aware of the importance of the very first impression you create on those considering you for the position being offered or for the part being cast. The moment you walk through the door, before uttering a word, a message is sent out by your attitude and appearance. Your body language speaks very loudly even when you are silent. So it is with a lector!

Procession

The way you stand, the way you walk in the procession, the way you hold the *Book of the Gospels* — all these create an immediate impression among assembly members. The role of lector does not begin with "A reading from. . . ." The poise and demeanor needed are often neglected in training programs.

If you walk in a slovenly manner as you process down the aisle, you are implying that you do not think highly of yourself or your ministry. Stand erect and hold the book reverently, as directed in your individual parish. Some hold the book chest-high, others elevate it only slightly. Never hold it directly in front of your face lest it impede your vision.

While on the subject of the procession, two things come to mind:

- First, the ladies' purses. Visiting a parish one Sunday, I noticed the lector processing with her purse hanging from her shoulder. It seemed it was the usual practice in this particular church, since no safe place was provided where ministers might deposit purses, keys, etc. I am well aware of the world in which we live and the fact that everyone attending Mass may not always be there to pray, but may fall prey to temptation. The pastor should provide all involved in the liturgy with a secure place to leave valuables. Purses are inappropriate hanging over a shoulder or dangling from the belt of a minister.

- Second, the carrying of the book from the sacristy, aside from the procession. The book is carried with such care and dignity when all are processing, but too often when the lector is walking to the back of the church where the procession starts, it is carried like yesterday's newspaper about to be discarded. It is still the book containing the word and deserves special respect when handled.

According to the latest revision of the General Instruction of the Roman Missal (GIRM 2000), if there is no deacon present, the lector carries the *Book of the Gospels* in the procession, holding it up somewhat and placing it on the altar. Before Mass the *Lectionary for Mass* is placed on the ambo. (I suggest it be left closed, for reasons that will be discussed shortly.) At the conclusion of the second reading, the lectionary is removed from the ambo and put in the place designated in the individual church. *No* book is carried in the recessional.

From the moment the celebrant begins the Mass, participate and respond to all prayers. Concentrate on where you are at that moment; do not be concerned with the readings at this point.

On Sundays, except during Lent and Advent, and on major feasts, the *Gloria* is said or sung. There is a concluding prayer spoken by the celebrant and then the altar server returns to his or her place after having held the Sacramentary for the priest. At Masses when the *Gloria* is omitted, the altar server returns at the conclusion of the Penitential Rite. At that point, the lector proceeds to the ambo for the first reading. Let the server, in returning to his or her chair, signal the end of the Introductory Rites and allow for the Liturgy of the Word to begin.

It may seem elementary to discuss the Mass and all its parts in such detail, but when new lectors are sitting in the sanctuary for the first few times, they are often intimidated and nerves can make them insecure as to what happens next; they cannot look to the congregation for direction — rather, the congregation is looking to them.

Always remember that liturgy should never be rushed. Take your time. Proceed to the ambo without haste, and when you are ready, open the book slowly and reverently. This is the time when the lectionary should be opened — opened to proclaim the word. This action is also a device to give you an opportunity to get yourself organized and to allow time for the congregation to be seated, put hymnals away and settle down to listen to the first reading. Opening the book at this point is profound since you are about to verbalize the word. Second, it gives you something to do and to fill, very gracefully, the time needed for you to compose yourself — to ask God's help in proclaiming his word, that you may read meaningfully and touch the congregation.

As a general rule, we do not deal well with silence and space. A few seconds with nothing to do seems an eternity; when your anticipation is heightened and you are anxious about any situation, you usually do not judge time accurately. In any form of performance situation, the feeling is even more exaggerated.

Opening and adjusting the book to avoid possible shadows caused by the microphone, etc., (which can be an annoyance and distracting) will fill the gap until you are ready, and when you are ready, the congregation will be ready. If you simply stand, looking into the congregation and waiting for the noise to subside, they can sense a negative attitude from some lectors by the expression on their faces. This is an immediate turn-off. If, however, you are very gracious and slow moving in your gestures, that space is filled gracefully and without having projected the feeling, "Well, when you people are quiet, then I'll begin."

What you are undertaking is a great responsibility. God is truly present in his word and you are about to have the extreme privilege of verbalizing his word and being the instrument that will bring it to life.

Proclamation

When you are prepared and ready to begin, let your eyes survey the entire congregation as you say, "A reading from. . . ." As you continue to read, it may or may not be possible for you to establish eye contact with the assembly members. Some readers find it difficult for their eyes to focus from the nearness of the book to the distant areas of the church and then refocus on the page. The most important aspects are the continuity of the scripture and communicating its message. If taking your eyes off the book creates a problem and interrupts the fluency and continuity of the text, then, very simply, do not attempt it.

Many moderators and priests training lectors emphasize the need for eye contact. Two things come into play here: first, the clergy are infinitely more familiar with the text than a layperson, and second, they are also more experienced in reading before the congregation — either or both of these make it easier for them to look away from the book than for the less experienced lector.

Also, eye contact means just that — establishing eye contact. How often readers take their eyes from the text and look to the ceiling, to a clock, the rear door or some other object! They do not look at the people; they look above or beyond. This serves no purpose. Some search out a familiar face in the congregation and constantly look to one person, if not one object. This also is pointless as it is not true *eye contact.*

Then we have the "peek-a-boo" look, in which the lector glances up fleetingly, looking at nothing or no one. The listeners are aware that this action is an obedient response to direction and one which serves no purpose, other than to make the lector appear nervous. Anxiety is picked up instantaneously by the assembly. Performers of all types must master the art of controlling nerves so that they are not visible to an audience. This is a subject we will delve into more fully in a later section of this book.

From my days as a pre-schooler, I have always been involved with broadcasting, radio as well as television, dealing with an unseen audience. I have always been able to sense an audience or congregation and feel their response to my message, whether in music or in speech. If you are fully prepared, convinced of the text and your delivery is strong, eye contact is not necessary. It is desirable and suggested but not mandatory. If it is disruptive to the scriptural passage and fragments it, it defeats its purpose. Therefore, if it disturbs you to look away from the book, then very simply, do not do it.

However, at two points, your eyes can and should embrace the entire community — at the outset as you say, "A reading from. . . ." and again at the finish of the passage as you conclude, "The word of the Lord."

Do not elaborate! When you begin, begin very simply: "A reading from. . . ." Television (commercials especially) is so redundant and explains the unnecessary so often that we frequently take this habit into our own lives and patterns. It is obvious that this is the *first* reading; it is not necessary and is somewhat degrading to the congregation to say, "The first reading today is a reading from. . . ." They are aware of the fact that it is the first reading. Don't pad your part!

During the readings, your hands should rest on the desk upon which the lectionary is placed, or on the bottom of the lectionary itself. Your arms should not be hanging at your sides while you read, totally separated from the podium. Again, body language. You are the medium through which these words are being brought to life, so in your body language it should be visible that you are connected to the book.

If you stand with your arms at your sides, you appear divorced from the book and the word you are proclaiming. A speaker delivering her own thoughts may stand in this fashion. Since you are verbalizing the Scripture, you are expressing thoughts and ideas contained in the lectionary. Therefore, it is only proper that you evidence a connection to it by the placement of your hands.

If the reading necessitates a page turn, prepare for it before you begin, so that you may avoid the possibility of turning more than one page. Turn the page quickly and quietly without disturbing the thought-line.

Be aware of the position of your head as the reading progresses to the bottom of the page. Often a lector's voice trails off and becomes distant and less audible at the bottom of the page, only to have the volume increase suddenly and tremendously at the page turn as the head is raised to accommodate the eye level for the text. As you progress to the bottom of the page, try sliding the lectionary up slightly, allowing your head to remain in the same position. This has a dual purpose: You maintain the same connection with the microphone and, consequently, the same volume level, and your neck is not too acutely bent so it will remain relaxed. If your chin drops toward your chest, the muscles of your neck tense and you can sense the tightening in your throat; consequently, the vocal timbre changes, becoming dull and lacking in quality, and so projection is impeded.

Always pause at the conclusion of a reading before adding, "The word of the Lord." This should not follow the final phrase as if it were the next sentence. Pause and embrace the entire community with your eyes and say very slowly and deliberately, "The word of the Lord." Otherwise, a lector may verbalize the phrase with the feeling, "Thank God, I got through it and it is over." We even hear it added as a throw away idea. Realize the meaning of the phrase and speak it accordingly.

If the psalm is being sung, return to your place; do not remain at the ambo if you are not reciting the psalm. In the General Instruction of the Roman Missal (GIRM) we learn that "at the lectern the reader proclaims the readings that precede the Gospel. If there is no cantor of the psalm, he [or she] may also sing or recite the responsorial psalm after the first reading" (150). In some churches, due to the architecture, it is not feasible to exit the ambo. If this is the case, step back from the book and turn to face the cantor singing the psalm. In this way, your attention is directed toward the person who is the focal point of the liturgy at that moment.

When you leave the ambo, do not turn your back to the tabernacle or the celebrant. If the Holy Father was celebrating the Mass, one would automatically face him, but sometimes we forget the little courtesies that should be employed.

Again, it is unnecessary to announce, "The responsorial psalm today is. . . ." Correctly, the *response* to the psalm is what the congregation will sing or recite; they do not read the verses of the psalm — the psalmist does, or in whose absence the cantor does, or in whose absence the lector does.

It is always wise to use your finger to indicate for yourself which verse you are reading. Then there will be no danger of skipping or repeating a verse when you take your eyes away from the page as you span the people to encourage them to join in the response.

If you are not speaking it, join in the singing of the refrain at the conclusion of each verse. At the end of the psalm, let the final notes fade and then some before getting up to do the second reading. In Masses without music when the lector reads the psalm, pause at the conclusion of the first reading to allow for a short meditation before beginning the response to the psalm. After pausing, read the refrain, then look at the congregation to invite them to respond. Your eyes are the invitation for them to respond to you, though sometimes they need a bit of prompting. Repeat this gesture of looking directly at the people at the conclusion of each verse. Vary the area of the church to which you look each time. In some parishes, the clergy may want a hand extended to cue assembly members. Follow the directions of your individual parish.

Whenever the Gospel acclamation is not sung, it is omitted. Never read the triple alleluia and verse. If there is no music, it is correctly omitted. Simply return to your place at the conclusion of the psalm or second reading. Weekday Masses usually have one reading and a psalm; Sunday and special feasts that occur on weekdays have two readings as well as a psalm.

At the completion of the second reading, your role as a lector is not finished. When the Gospel has been read and the celebrant is delivering his homily, participate by listening. Sometimes I think we have forgotten the *art* of listening. Due, I am sure, to the redundancy of television, we have lost this art. If it is a news item, it is flashed across the screen several times an hour and the same applies to the warning of an impending storm. It is almost impossible to count the times we are assailed with the very same commercial in the course of one evening. So we have developed the art of ignoring! Somewhere along the line, we have forgotten to listen and really hear a message because we realize it will be repeated so often. Listening takes concentration, and concentration demands self-discipline. This discipline to continue to concentrate and consequently to hear (especially over a prolonged period of time such as a homily) is attainable, if we just work at it.

Just as the celebrant and possibly the deacon were attentive to you as you proclaimed the Scripture, so too must your attention be directed toward the homilist. Granted, not everyone is a brilliant and exciting preacher. Some write beautifully and have a great gift for composing beautiful ideas and thoughts that would be very moving if delivered by a more dynamic speaker. Everyone is not blessed with the talent for content and the ability to impart these messages in a meaningful way. Whether the homily is being given with dynamism or the homilist is really struggling, you must be attentive.

When seated in the altar area, keep both feet flat on the floor with knees together. Legs must never be crossed in a position one might assume while relaxing and watching television. Sit erect and look attentive. Model good body language.

Prayer of the Faithful

At the conclusion of the creed, if there is no deacon present, the General Intercessions (Prayer of the Faithful) may be read by the lector. The GIRM states "After the priest gives the introduction to the general intercessions, the reader may announce the intentions when no deacon is present" (151). Depending on the sources used, these petitions can be more awkward than the readings. Since they are not usually available until just prior to Mass, this is one of the last-minute items that must be prepared in the all-too-brief fifteen minutes before Mass.

Proceed to the ambo as soon as the creed is completed and stand, ready to start, while the celebrant reads the introductory phrases. You should not be in motion during these beginning sentences.

Included in the intercessions are the names of the sick and recently deceased. Be sure to check the names prior to Mass. I am certain everyone has had the painful experience of being at a Mass at which the name of a relative or close friend has been announced. Nothing is more disturbing than hearing the name of someone you love among the deceased and it is all the more upsetting to hear the name mispronounced!

I would suggest the obituary column of the local newspaper be consulted to practice reading names that are unusual or of nationalities foreign to your own. This is an excellent source for practicing the pronunciation of various ethnic sounds.

If you have lived in the parish for any length of time, you are aware of its particular character. The sacristan is often familiar with funerals that are current and could possibly help you with the proper pronunciation. Otherwise, consult one of the priests. Above all, do not guess. Do not be ashamed to ask and do not assume you know the correct pronunciation.

At the conclusion of the petitions, remain standing in exactly the same position. Wait until the celebrant has concluded the final passages of the intercessions before you move the book or the binder from which you read. Any movement is disruptive. Often, people do not realize that their actions are inappropriate. If someone is speaking, whatever the circumstances, it is rude to move or in any way distract from what is being said. Your last petition does not conclude the intercessory prayers; therefore, remain standing, focused on the text that the priest is reading. Then, return to your place.

Your role as a lector is not complete although you may have completed the readings. The lector should be ready and able to join in reciting all parts of the

Mass. If you do not know all the prayers by memory, use the missal or whatever booklets your parish provides. In any case, visibly join in all parts of the Mass, spoken or sung. You need not have an exceptional voice to join in the singing. The Lord appreciates your efforts, regardless of your talent. Remember, he knows of your abilities and limitations; it is he who gave them to you.

Liturgy of the Eucharist

Realize that the congregation does not identify with the clergy. The celebrant is a priest and as such, is not one of the laity. The lector, however, is a layperson and so is "one of them." The actions and demeanor of lectors, cantors, altar servers and special eucharistic ministers are very significant, and for many in the congregation they are role models. Therefore, the action of the lector throughout Mass is vitally important.

Whenever there is even a suggestion of a papal visit, excitement starts to build. People clamor for tickets and if you are fortunate enough to secure one, you become one of thousands in the assembly. For security reasons as well as accessibility to the space where Mass will be celebrated, you must arrive hours ahead to find your seat. This could possibly be far enough away to make the Holy Father appear to be a tiny image, so small as to make watching painfully difficult. Yet we strive to obtain a ticket, wait patiently for Mass to begin, sometimes in very inclement weather and the enthusiasm mounts to fever pitch with the first strains of the opening anthem.

Understand this, please. I do not mean to downplay or in any way denigrate a papal visit. I certainly realize the Holy Father is the Vicar of Christ, and for most people a papal visit is a once-in-a-lifetime experience. If you have viewed a papal Mass on television, the intimacy of the camera allows you to see the undivided attention given by all in attendance; they are positively in awe. That is as it should be.

However, we have the opportunity to participate in Mass every day, so perhaps we take it for granted. It really does not matter if the celebrant is the Holy Father or a "father who is less than holy." When he takes common, ordinary bread and wine and utters the words of Christ and, through the miracle of transubstantiation, changes them into his body and blood, the priest celebrant is, indeed, another Christ.

At a papal Mass everyone watches in rapt attention. How often we passively follow our distractions or pay little heed to the magnificence of Christ's gift to us!

Have you ever imagined what it would have been like to have been with the apostles at the Last Supper, thought how blessed they were or even envied them? Imagine what the apostles must have felt when they shared the Passover meal with our Lord and took part in the institution of the Eucharist. We are invited in faith to share this experience constantly. Sometimes we do not accept the invitation or do not avail ourselves of the wonderful gift. Occasionally we fail to open ourselves or cooperate fully with God's grace.

We are privileged to witness Jesus Christ as the priest celebrant shows him to us after uttering, "This is my body. This is my blood." We see what transpired as our Lord instituted the priesthood and empowered the apostles and all those called to follow after them when he said, "Do this in memory of me."

What an incredibly wonderful gift the One, Holy, Catholic and Apostolic Faith is! How sad that we sometimes take it for granted or fail to appreciate it! Depths of faith seem to vary as much as the depths of the ocean — so shallow at the shoreline and deepening only as you go farther into it.

In 1994 a study sponsored by the *New York Times* and the Columbia Broadcasting System regarding the attitudes and beliefs held by Catholics concerning the Eucharist indicated that many Catholics do not believe in the Real Presence. The poll showed that in the United States roughly two adult Catholics out of three believe that bread and wine are *merely symbolic*. The figures were:

> 70% for ages 18–44
> 58% for ages 45–64
> 45% for ages 65 and older

Apparently, this poll was not taken among "fallen-away" or "lapsed" Catholics but among those who attend Mass regularly. I wonder how lectors would fare if such a poll was taken among them.

Lectoring is such a privilege and an opportunity to deepen one's faith. The philosopher and theologian Romano Guardini said, "Faith is the ability to live with a doubt." Consider it for a moment — if there is no doubt, there is certainty; hence there is no need for faith.

It is truly an honor to be a lector, to stand within feet of the altar and to be in such proximity to the very epitome of our faith and lives. It is almost impossible to be untouched by Christ's presence. I say, "almost," because we must cooperate with his grace if we are to be moved by it.

Perhaps if one falls into the category of the *New York Times* poll, being a lector might be a good reason to question one's own thinking and probe more deeply into one's own soul and ask God's help for vision. What you feel is what you reflect and consequently, what the congregation senses. Granted, we are human beings, and as such, have human weaknesses. We are all easily distracted and our minds tend to wander, particularly in a solitary situation such as prayer. As humans, we find it sometimes easier and sometimes more difficult to concentrate and respond. This, too, is something that can be worked on and improved.

Realize that the lector holds a very special part in the liturgy. Regardless of how many priests may be present at a Mass, the lector is a layperson, not one of the clergy. At a papal Mass, with hundreds of deacons, priests, bishops, even cardinals present, the lector is still one of the laity.

Prior to the Second Vatican Council, altar boys or choir members had the special privilege of being the only lay participants in the Mass. Vatican II changed all that, and members of the laity now have the opportunity to be ministers of welcome, ministers of the word, extraordinary ministers of the Eucharist, altar servers and cantors. Younger people among us are perhaps unable to fully appreciate what that means since they were not even born when females were allowed in the altar area only for baptism, confirmation, Eucharist and marriage or if they ventured beyond the altar rail to clean. We have come so far since the sixties that we often forget, or are totally unaware of, how different it was. At most Masses the priest celebrant walked directly onto the altar area; his vestments included the biretta (hat with ridges). Accompanied by two altar *boys,* he turned his back on the congregation to face the altar, which was against the wall, and proceeded to say Mass in Latin, a language incomprehensible to most. The congregation witnessed and followed along with their missals, flipping pages back and forth from the ordinary parts of the Mass to the propers. There was no opportunity to participate personally as we do today.

I sometimes think those old enough to remember have forgotten and younger people are unaware of how difficult it was for many to involve themselves fully at Mass. It is a unique opportunity and privilege for us to be ministers and to participate actively, consciously and fully at Mass.

In Conclusion

I have spent a great deal of time discussing the lector as a person. This is, no doubt, a carry-over from my own private teaching. I find it impossible to teach someone how to sing if I have not touched that person first.

A voice is a God-given instrument encased in a human being. All that a human being is — everything — is reflected in the voice. The body, soul, mind and personality combined are parts of that voice. It is mandatory to realize that any singer or speaker is totally involved, employing more than just little bands of tissue in the larynx. The body, mind and, yes, soul too, are a unity and come into play as one when words are expressed. One of my coaches affiliated with the Metropolitan Opera strongly claimed, "A singer's soul is on exhibition," and I agree.

The voice is a mirror reflecting a person's innermost being and personality; its quality, rate and pitch alter as emotions alter. Anger, elation, depression, anxiety — we could go on — all are displayed as we use our voices.

So, indeed, the voice is the person and the person is the voice.

PART TWO: TECHNIQUE

Posture

A starving nation could be fed on the amount of money spent in this country on diet foods and diet fads in an attempt to appear slimmer. Memberships in health clubs and gyms run into countless millions each year. We work so hard at trying to look better, yet we overlook the obvious — posture.

There is a very easy solution and an immediate way to visually lose about ten pounds. Stand up straight. The scale will not vary but the appearance will, if the posture is improved. Unfortunately, we have become very slovenly about our stance, though we drink diet sodas and work out at the gym in an attempt to fit into smaller sizes.

A costly outfit will look better on the hanger if the posture is bad, whereas inexpensive attire can look "like a million dollars" if carried correctly. Carriage is mandatory to look alert and alive and to portray a sense of self-confidence. The way you stand speaks loudly about your personality. Your mood and general attitude are reflected in the way you carry yourself.

In a joyous song by Leonard Bernstein, lyricists Betty Comden and Adolph Green effused, "I could touch the sky!" That is true; when things are going well for us, we stand tall and feel as if we could touch the sky itself. On the other hand, when we are unhappy or depressed we tend to slouch. Depending on the posture, a feeling of assurance or a look of apology or inadequacy is conveyed without a word being uttered.

If you walk around the Lincoln Center area in New York, it is always interesting to watch the young hopefuls scurrying to lessons, classes and rehearsals. It is fun to try to determine whether they are involved in drama, instrumental music, voice or dance. Dancers are always obvious, not only because of their turn-out (the angle of the feet when walking) but primarily because their posture is the most erect, followed by singers. When we develop proper bearing, as performers do, it becomes automatic, second nature. But first, we must develop a conscious awareness of our bodies. Working on this is a "must" if you are to breathe correctly. The primary purpose of good posture is not to look better, but to enable us to use the breathing mechanism to its fullest potential. As with many other aspects of life, if it looks better, it works better.

Proper bearing does not mean posing stiffly. If you are standing correctly, an imaginary straight line can be drawn from your ear, to your shoulder, to your hip, to your heel.

- If your head is held high and erect, atop your spine and your chin is not jutting forward or, conversely, pulled back, then your ear and shoulder will be aligned.

- If your torso is straight, not bending forward at the waist or with your chest collapsed, then your shoulders and hips are aligned.

- If your body weight is focused forward on the balls of your feet (without bent knees) then your hips and heels will be aligned.

Therefore, we have that imaginary line: ear, shoulder, hip and heel.

Now let us reverse the entire process. Start at the floor. The body weight should be on the balls of the feet — not settled back into the heels, which causes slouching. Weight should be equally distributed on both feet; do not favor one foot, or you will find yourself shifting back and forth. When the body is focused forward, the heels touch the floor lightly, giving the body a feeling of lifting. Indeed, lift yourself up out of your hips.

Many teachers use the following imagery. If its purpose and concept are not clearly understood, it is meaningless.

Just for a moment, imagine yourself to be a marionette with a string coming out of your head and your entire body suspended from above. This gives a feeling of lifting up and encourages the proper situation for inhalation. Even the head is erect as it should be. You must consciously lift yourself up, out of your hips; in other words, elongate the area between your rib cage and your hips. In adopting this stance, the rib cage extends at the floating ribs which allows the breath to fill at the base of the lungs. Liquid poured unimpeded into a bottle goes immediately to the bottom; so it is with the air you inhale. With an expanded rib cage, breath is unimpeded and can reach the base of the lungs to permit deeper breathing. Try this little puppet experiment; I promise it works.

Here is another exercise I find helpful. Stand, feet slightly apart, and extend your arms over your head. Reach up (as ballerinas do) with palms facing inward, fingers relaxed, elbows slightly bent and shoulders relaxed. While in this position, be aware of the lift you feel in the rib cage, and the widening of the space between the edge of the ribs at your sides and your hip bones. Be conscious of the flatness in the diaphragm area and the abdomen. Your heels should be barely touching the ground with your body weight on the balls of the feet. *Slowly,* let your arms return to their normal position, being aware, as you do so, of maintaining the feeling of tallness and the widening of the floating ribs.

Repeat this a few times, conscious of your torso. Be very aware of the position of your body, particularly the rise and extension in your rib area. Each time you lower your arms, concentrate on keeping the same extension in the upper torso and flatness in the abdominal area. This posture is absolutely mandatory for correct breathing and is strongly advised for the betterment of appearance. To repeat, the primary purpose is not for appearance, but rather to set up the proper conditions for correct breathing.

This may be far from the normal stance for *you*, but it *is* the normal, correct one. Pupils will often complain that something is uncomfortable. "Uncomfortable" is the wrong word. Questioned further, they add, "Nothing hurts but it's just uncomfortable." My response is always the same: "The word is *different*." Because it is a position to which the person is unaccustomed, it does indeed feel strange. In time, it will become natural and eventually, second nature.

Sometimes, in a misguided sense of modesty, people bring their shoulders forward, collapsing the chest. This is neither modesty nor piety. It is a confused contradiction of all that God intends in creating the magnificent machine called the respiratory system. Others are guilty of leaning forward at the waist. Even singers are prone to this, though they should be the last ones to fall into this category. I often think that this position is caused by the individual's subconscious attempt to reach the listener. This is very prevalent when a speaker or singer is on a platform. For some reason, they seem to feel they are communicating more personally if they bend toward the listeners. However, if you watch concert or opera singers leaning forward, observing them carefully, you will notice that they lean forward at the level of the hips. This keeps the waist area straight — the diaphragm and all that needs to expand are not collapsed — and does not impede proper breath support. Bending forward at the waist defeats correct breathing.

To check the validity of this concept, perform this experiment. With your hands (fingers front) around the ribs, bend forward slightly at the waist and feel the bony structure pressing into the flesh and preventing the expansion of the lungs at the base. This is where breath support is focused if there is to be proper projection of tone in speech or song.

In conclusion, I suggest a little trick that I propose to my students who are striving to eliminate a specific problem. Being creatures of habit, we all tend to regress into our old ways of doing things and need some reminder to help us think about whatever problem we are attempting to eradicate. Change the way you wear your watch. If it is usually worn on your left wrist, switch it to the right wrist. Every time you check the hour, finding your watch relocated will serve as a reminder: "Stand up straight!" It is impossible to estimate the number of times each day when there will be the split-second thought "posture." This is far more beneficial than ignoring your posture for days and thinking about it only when you are at the ambo.

This brief, though constant, reminder is so much more efficient. Eventually, it works and you will find your stature has changed for the better. Just do not expect it to happen immediately. Be persistent and persevere; you will find this "new look" to be an advantage in everything you do. Posture will not be right at the ambo unless it is right at all times. For posture, breathing, delivery and projection to be effective, they must be a part of you and not something you turn on with, "A reading from. . . ."

Breathing

"The Lord God formed man out of the clay of the ground and blew into his nostrils the breath of life, and man became a living being."
— Genesis 2:7

Breath is life. It is the first thing we do when we enter this world and it is the last thing we do when we leave it.

With correct stance, we set up the proper conditions for the respiration needed for speech or song. The normal tidal breathing that is automatic and suffices for general conversation will never supply our needs for any form of public speaking or singing. Two differences separate the breath needed for lectoring from the breath needed for conversational speech: the limited time for inhaling and the greater demand for the extension of breath, over a longer time.

In normal conversation, the pace is unconsciously varied because of content, emotion, the speaker's personality etc. However, the readings are quite another matter. More volume is needed; the pace must be slower to accommodate the acoustics of the church and to allow for comprehension of the message imparted. The sentence structure is often very involved and sometimes awkward. Breath must be taken in quickly and spun out over long and difficult sentences. Interrupting clauses to snatch a breath can be ruinous to the meaning. So we must learn to inhale quickly and exhale slowly. It sounds so simple, doesn't it?

If you want to observe breathing done perfectly, using the entire system to its fullest, watch a dog or any other animal. I am not being facetious! I have always had a toy poodle, and on many occasions have used my tiny pet to demonstrate to my students how naturally and correctly breathing can be done. Even while the animal sleeps, you will notice where the expansion is centered as it breathes, fully using the base of the lungs for proper depth of breath.

Observe when the dog barks. My little five-pounder can be heard at a great distance, as can most dogs. When he barks his front paws actually leave the floor as his hind quarters contract to support the breath. Even his tail pulls downward as he engages in "canine conversation."

We are awed by the engineering and mechanism of expensive cars and marvel at their design and construction. Yet we rarely stop to marvel at the construction of our bodies, designed and created by the master builder himself, God.

If we may briefly refresh ideas we learned in a basic anatomy course — the rib cage consists of twelve pairs of ribs, attached in front to the sternum or breast bone and in back to the spine. The two bottom-most pairs are commonly called "floating ribs" as they are unattached in front, though they are connected to the spine in the back.

It may seem that we have discussed various parts of the respiratory system and have omitted that which is commonly *thought to be* of central importance: the lungs. On the contrary, in breathing the lungs are completely passive. It is really the muscles that are responsible for getting additional air into the lungs quickly and adequately to support a tone, spoken or sung.

The intercostals are those muscles between the ribs which lift them, thereby increasing the diameter of the chest. Most importantly, the principal muscle involved is the diaphragm.

The diaphragm consists of muscular fibers; dome-shaped, it forms the floor for the respiratory system and the ceiling for the digestive mechanism. If you are not sure where your diaphragm is, pay attention the next time you have the hiccoughs. Hiccoughs are actually spasms of the diaphragm and a prolonged bout of them creates a soreness that will bother you when you use this muscle to support your tone. The diaphragm is the main muscle of inspiration. When its dome contracts, the central tendon is pulled down, which widens the thorax.

We hear people say, "Breathe with your stomach." However, the stomach has nothing to do with breath. It is a major organ of the digestive system and, as we discussed, is separated from the respiratory mechanism by the diaphragm. People wrongly refer to the abdomen as the stomach. Perhaps the confusion about breathing with the stomach comes from the fact that the abdominal muscles are very involved in the support system: They support the breath to support the tone, spoken or sung.

Another common misconception is that a deep breath means lifting the shoulders. Just the contrary! Shoulders must be relaxed at all times and remain out of the breathing process.

Just envision for a moment! A deep breath means just that — *deep* — the air will reach into the base of the lungs if these floating ribs extend, as God intended, expanding all the way back to the spine.

Relaxation for Inspiration

Try a little experiment. As you read this, raise and lower your shoulders. Do not do it in synchronization with breathing. Raise the shoulders high and then relax them, letting them drop. As you lift them, be aware of all the tension you feel in your shoulders, your upper arms as well as the neck area.

Let us try a different experiment. This one you can see as well as sense. Make a fist and notice how the arm muscles react. The hand is not solely involved, rather, you can see and feel the tensing all the way up to the upper arm. So it is with your throat. If shoulders are raised, the neck and throat muscles also tense, so it is impossible for the voice not to react as well. The tightening produces a pinched and unpleasant quality, and the range of the speaking voice is more limited.

Once again, raise your shoulders, noticing how much energy it takes, and then drop them completely, being aware of the delightful sense of relaxation, including your neck and back. Repeat this motion, but this time, try to relax even more. Ask yourself if you can't free these muscles just a bit more. Remember — any unnecessary tension is wasted energy that should be directed toward the job at hand. Remember too, you can raise and lower your shoulders without breathing and you can breathe without raising and lowering your shoulders.

Go back to the marionette idea. Assume that erect posture of lifting up out of your hips, of feeling suspended from above. Place your hands gently around the bottom of your rib cage — thumbs in front and fingers reaching around to your spine. As you inhale, be aware of the expansion of the floating ribs; they should be pushing your hands outward. The intake of air filling the base of the lungs forces the finger tips of both hands farther apart. You should realize that this expansion goes all the way around to the spine. As the breath is exhaled, the lungs empty and the ribs contract. Consequently, the hands return to a more closed position, as at the start. This expansion of the rib cage for fuller, deeper breathing is absolutely essential and must be developed and mastered.

Think for a moment. Haven't we all played with a ball at some time or other — bouncing it and trying to make it go higher each time? In an attempt to achieve greater height, it was necessary to hit it harder into the pavement to give it greater impetus to reach greater heights. In other words, the ball hits the ground harder to travel farther. So it is with breath. For the voice to project more, the breath and the whole support system must reach down farther than what is needed for general conversation.

We have discussed the freedom needed in the shoulder area. It is easy to realize that no container can be easily filled with any substance if there is any type of restriction at or near its aperture. So it is with the mouth and throat; if the tongue and pharyngeal area are tensed, not only will breathing be impeded and the quality lessened but it will also be noisy. Just as the shoulders were relaxed, it is also mandatory that the throat be relaxed to permit a greater intake of air. If the pharynx is tightened, breathing will be noisy, which is particularly disconcerting when amplification is involved.

Did you ever play a little game of reaching into a jar of marbles or jelly beans, taking out a handful and seeing who would get the greatest amount? The winner would always be the player whose hand went into the container wide opened and relaxed, and whose fingers closed gently and easily, without grabbing. This brought out a fist full of jelly beans or marbles. The person whose hand went in tensely, and who grabbed at the contents, emerged with surprisingly few candies. The same is true of breath. If the whole mechanism is relaxed and the throat is opened freely, the air will pass quickly and quietly into the lungs, and with practice the capacity for breath will increase.

Breath that is literally grabbed, that is taken tensely, is always insufficient. Another important and unpleasant side effect is that the throat is dried out by this action, which is always a detriment to speakers and singers.

It is a proven fact that a great percentage of the manifestation of tension is focused in and around the mouth, jaw and neck area. In actuality, we must work very hard to "try not to try" — in other words, we have to make a definite effort to overcome the natural tendency to tighten in this area.

Nasal breathing is always wiser and healthier but not always feasible. The nose is lined in such a fashion that the air is warmed and filtered before it reaches the throat. However, the mouth provides a much larger orifice and allows for a greater intake of air that consequently can be taken more quickly. This is necessary for any form of public speaking.

The human body is such a magnificent work of God, and it is such a tightly geared system — each part dependent upon another and interacting to produce the end result. If the support system is not working properly and the breath is not adequate enough to allow for the proper action of the vocal cords, the tone is breathy because the cords are not approximating correctly, allowing the escape of air. It could be said that the tone is "wrapped up in breath." However, when the entire system is working to its fullest — supporting muscles working to send the breath to the larynx so that the vocal cords approximate securely — the tone is clear because all the air is converted to sound and not wasted. In this case, we might say the breath is *under* the voice instead of *through* it. A breathy tone is a sultry sound and not an appropriate quality for proclaiming the Scriptures. Even more importantly, it is not healthy because the cords are approximating incorrectly, allowing escaping breath. Over a prolonged period of time, this can lead to medical problems.

Breathing Exercises

Stand in your "marionette" position. Focus your attention during these exercises on the mid-section of your body. It is helpful to stand before a mirror and watch the activities of these muscles involved in respiration.

Place your right hand on your chest, slightly lower than a choker or a tie would rest. The left hand is placed just above the waist. This creates an awareness of the movement of the muscles responsible for proper breathing, necessary for public speaking or song. The right hand should hardly move, and in time, not move at all. Movement beneath the right hand would indicate the inadvisable high chest breathing. The left hand should feel the in and out movement that accompanies deep breathing. It goes without saying at this point; the shoulders should be completely relaxed and motionless.

Breathe easily, being conscious of the action of the mechanism. Relax a bit — inhale, hold for a moment, exhale, counting to five. Repeat, counting to six, and so on. This is very important! At first, do this only twice and then pause to relax. Gradually, you can increase the counts and the number of times the exercise is repeated. If you are over-zealous and try to do too much too soon, you will hyper-ventilate. Give your body a chance to adjust to the changes in the blood chemistry and proceed slowly, or you will find yourself becoming dizzy.

Another very different position to try this new concept in breathing is to try all this lying down. A prone position is very beneficial in that it is not conducive to shoulder involvement. In fact, it makes it almost impossibly difficult to keep raising the shoulders, thereby employing high-chest breathing. In this position, place your right hand on your upper abdomen. Feel your hand being pushed out as you inhale. Take a breath, hold it for a moment, and exhale suddenly as if blowing out candles on a cake. Feel the sudden reaction as the abdomen and diaphragm area contract under your hand, being aware of the fact that this is your support system at work. As we have discussed, these abdominal muscles, as well as the diaphragm, pull in and support the breath, which in turn supports the voice.

For another standing marionette idea, place your hands around the rib cage, finger tips to the back, and as you inhale, be conscious of the outward movement of the ribs against your hands as you take a truly deep breath.

A different position for extending the rib cage is to stand with your hands behind your head. Do not allow the shoulders to come forward when trying this. You will tire quickly with your arms upward; when this happens, try a different position to avoid tension.

When you are more comfortable with these exercises and the muscles are more controlled, try this process while walking with your arms relaxed at your sides. Walk and breathe rhythmically. Walking at your usual pace, inhale through your nose (this is especially important if you are doing this outdoors) and exhale over three or four steps, repeat, then relax and breathe normally for a few paces. Repeat the entire process, increasing the steps for exhaling. In time, you might find it pleasant if you "Whistle a Happy Tune" or hum instead of counting. Whistling has another purpose; it promotes flexibility of the lips.

If nothing else, these very basic exercises should create an awareness of "which muscles are doing what" during proper inhalation with support for phonation.

Many people may be unfamiliar with the name Gioacchino Rossini. But no one is unfamiliar with some of his compositions, particularly the famous "William Tell Overture" and the ever-popular opera, *The Barber of Seville.* The maestro supposedly commented that there are two ways of breathing — good and bad! Indeed, I would not dispute that idea with anyone, particularly anyone so eminent as Rossini.

Delivery

Pacing

I have found that learning the correct tempo or rate of speech is one of the most difficult aspects for lectors. It has rarely been necessary for me to correct a lector for reading too slowly. The normal conversational rate is not appropriate for the proclamation of the Scripture.

Delivering a speech for a political campaign or a classroom assignment is also different, because of the size of the room and the weight of the text. The acoustics and size of a church determine the pace, as does the message to be imparted. Some paragraphs from the *Encyclopedia Britannica* could be more easily absorbed than Revelation or some passages of Saint Paul.

It is totally impossible to give any true sense of pacing in a book. This changes in every instance due to the acoustics of the church. Every building differs in size, shape and reverberations (or lack thereof). Therefore, guidance in this area must come locally from the individual parish, preferably from the clergy who are certainly familiar with the situation and experienced in dealing with it.

The congregation must not only be able to hear the reading — they must be able to digest it. If the words are coming too rapidly, they tend to choke the listeners. We might liken it to eating an apple. You cannot bite, bite, bite an apple without allowing for chewing and swallowing each bite, or you would choke. So it is with any form of public speaking. The ideas should not be given any faster then they can be absorbed and digested or they are valueless. The assembly should not just hear words; they should hear the message and digest it.

Whether you are proclaiming Scripture, having a conversation or singing an aria or hymn, articulate clearly. People who speak too quickly tend to be careless in their enunciation. Consequently, the message is muddled and difficult to understand.

One of the greatest problems with speaking too quickly is that it usually means words are not enunciated properly. The three major organs of articulation — the lips, the tongue, and the soft palate — must be given the necessary time to do their jobs, to shape the vowels accurately and sharply form all consonants. Often, multi-syllabic words suffer most because the person neglects to speak every syllable clearly. Many of us are guilty of slurring and omitting parts of words, especially word endings.

So often after correcting a pupil who is half-pronouncing a word, when the vowel sound is true and consonants fully voiced, the person senses so much more activity on the part of the articulators, particularly the tongue. This gives the student a realization of how neglectful the lips and tongue have been. Whether it is speech or song, it matters not; the tempo should never exceed a pace at which every part of a word or every note can be clearly articulated. Blurred sound is never effective or understandable.

If you are driving on a strange, curvy and dark road, you wisely and automatically slow down to retain control of the car and to avoid an accident due to an unfamiliar roadbed. Some foolish people maintain speed and the consequences can be unfortunate. The same applies to lectors: As in driving, there are many reasons for varying the speed.

If you find a certain word hard to pronounce, use it in a way that will avoid the difficulty. Leaning on the word requires a slightly slower pace in order to enunciate more deliberately and carefully. This will prevent running ahead and mispronouncing the troublesome word. If you do it very purposefully, it will work *for* you rather than being a stumbling block. The trick is to make it sound as if you *want* to shape the phrase in this fashion, rather than have it apparent that it is being done thusly out of necessity. For example, in the "old" lectionary we had one passage in particular that tripped many lectors. In my first year of training them, the moderator of the lectors warned me prior to the practice session, "Just be sure they do not say smoking brassieres!" When I began working on that passage, it did pose a problem. I did what I usually do with problem words; in the lectors' practice books I wrote the word phonetically *(bray' zher)* above it. My suggestion to all of them was the same: slow the tempo of the entire preceding line, which affords an opportunity to anticipate the word, preparing to pronounce it accurately.

This is the passage, Second Sunday of Lent C (27):

When the sun had set and it was dark, there appeared a smoking brazier and a flaming torch, which passed between those pieces.

Many are thankful the passage has been changed in the new lectionary. The line now reads: **"there appeared a smoking fire pot and a flaming torch."**

Those who have a naturally faster rate of speaking will really find it necessary to apply the brakes when lectoring. For them, the slower tempo will seem strange indeed. They will require constant reminders to accustom themselves to a slower tempo. It takes quite some time to implement new ideas and techniques before one can be completely confident of mastery. Many times, what is meant by "speaking slowly" is misunderstood. Some people read at a fairly rapid pace and then pause too long at commas and periods. This disrupts ideas and fragments sentences.

Imagine two cars are driving along an avenue. One drives fast and is forced to wait longer at the red lights; the other goes at a more comfortable speed, approaches each light just as it is turning green, pausing only slightly. This pattern can continue for quite a stretch, and what happens at the end of the avenue? Both cars arrive at the spot simultaneously with the racer having accomplished nothing but wearing out his brakes. The smooth drive is far more satisfying and comfortable. It is the same with the readings. If pauses are too long, the fluidity is disturbed. Elongated or frequent pauses are not the same as slower pacing.

The tempo at which one reads varies in many ways. First, it is a personal item; everyone's pacing is unique. Each of us has a habitual or average rate of walking, talking and eating. The basic pace of speech should vary, depending upon a great number of factors, including the topic, the emotion, the acoustics and, most importantly, the formality of the occasion.

There is really no set rate of speech. Every person, every language, every emotion, every situation demands something different. If we stop for a moment and think about it, we will realize that we were created subject to minute, yet tremendous physical changes as we react to all types of stimuli.

The heart rate and respiration react according to our activities. Even sitting quietly, watching a movie, as the tension and excitement mount, the heart beats faster. This is a natural response in everyone. It is the same with speech. We do not normally speak as if we had built-in metronomes. Different lectors read at different rates. If they all read the same, the readings will be stilted, unnatural and awkward.

Changing tempo within a reading is reserved for the more experienced lector or one who has a background in acting or public speaking. Altering speed is subtle and usually is not recognized as such by the listeners. They know this particular lector is better, but often they are unable to articulate why they think so. I do not encourage the average lector to try tempo variations. As with a skilled musician, the discipline needed must be mastered or the pace will accelerate and not return to the original tempo. In other words, the reading will continually run ahead like a sled going downhill.

Subtle, and some not-so-subtle, variations in rate are as necessary in speech as rubato is in music. A simple way to understand this principle is to consider a tree in the breeze. It stands straight and tall until the wind starts to blow. Then it bends back and forth gracefully until the wind stops and it is again upright. However, if there is a fierce, hurricane-like gale that forces it too far, it bends, breaks and is ruined. So it is with tempo changes. Any deviation should be temporary, and at its conclusion, the original should be resumed. The experienced person who reads the story of creation (Genesis 1:1 — 2:2) employing this technique really brings it to life.

Then God said:

"Let us make man in our image,
     after our likeness."

And again:

God created man in his image;
     in the image of God he created him;
     male and female he created them.
God blessed them, saying:
"Be fertile and multiply;
     fill the earth and subdue it."

These passages certainly demand to be slower than:

God made all kinds of wild animals,
     all kinds of cattle,
and all kinds of creeping things of the
     earth.

And again:

> **"Let them have dominion over the fish of**
> **the sea, the birds of the air and the**
> **cattle, and over all the wild animals**
> **and all the creatures that crawl on**
> **the ground."**

"Man," God's ultimate creation in his own image, needs to be slower to emphasize the importance of the line. The reference to man's creation occurs twice. It would seem wise to make the second slightly slower and more emphatic than the first. Also draw on the redundancy of the phrase, "Evening came, and morning followed." This should have the same pace and inflection each time. Note the difference in the pattern for the seventh day:

> **"Since on the seventh day God was finished**
> **with the work he had been doing,**
> **he rested on the seventh day from all the**
> **work he had undertaken."**

One of the greatest problems in having long intervals between lector assignments is the loss of a sense of timing. In a church with fewer lectors who read more frequently, they are more easily able to maintain the feeling for an appropriate tempo. However, if there has been a period of several weeks, they return to the ambo like novices, and for many reasons the pacing they had developed eludes them, and the words tend to accelerate.

Be aware of the need to concentrate on slowing the pace after a prolonged absence from lectoring. Very few lectors embrace a slow tempo automatically. Nerves, emotions and the frenetic lifestyle that most of us lead, are all contributing factors that encourage the reader to run ahead.

For some reason which I have always failed to comprehend, readings which are very long or very short tend to create a feeling of urgency and lectors hurry through these passages. The long readings, I can understand, but I can find no reason for hastening a short one. It does not matter whether you are narrating the Passion on Palm Sunday or the short, beautiful passage from the Book of Numbers on January 1st; nothing should be rushed. All of it is the word of the Lord and proclaiming it too rapidly renders it ineffective.

Phrasing

A related thought that needs to be discussed at this point is phrasing: the process which takes words, binds them together and converts them into messages. In speech or in song, we phrase for two reasons. The first is necessity; phrasing allows us to breathe and breathes life into words. Since breath is life, we might say that phrasing makes words come alive. Second, we phrase for interpretive purposes, in order to make sentences more meaningful. Lectors must learn to shape a phrase or a sentence just the same as singers do. In vocal music, there is a marriage of lyric and music provided by the composer; in most spoken texts, it is left up to the person delivering the script to decide the best places to pause and breathe and, consequently, to phrase.

When I was a freshman in high school, we had a drama coach who used to go to all classes, teaching us how to read poetry. I have a vivid remembrance of one of my classmates beginning to read Joyce Kilmer's poem, "Trees." She began:

"I think that I shall never see — *pause* —
A poem lovely as a tree."

Immediately the teacher stopped her rather abrasively, asking, "What is wrong with you? Are you blind?" We were all mystified when she repeated, "Are you blind? What shall you never see? You must continue into the next line:

'I think that I shall never see

A poem — *pause* — lovely as a tree.' "

It made a lasting impression on me. I wonder if the girl involved remembers the incident.

We readers often face the matter of phrasing, particularly in the psalms when the cantor or psalmist is absent (GIRM, 36, 66). Because we come to the end of a line does not mean the thought ends and a breath or pause is needed. I have always thought the psalms often require more preparation time than the readings. The wordage, and especially the structure, are far from what one would find in ordinary prose. Think of the message to be conveyed. Practice and plan where the appropriate pauses should be — not necessarily at the end of each line.

Key for Practice Passages

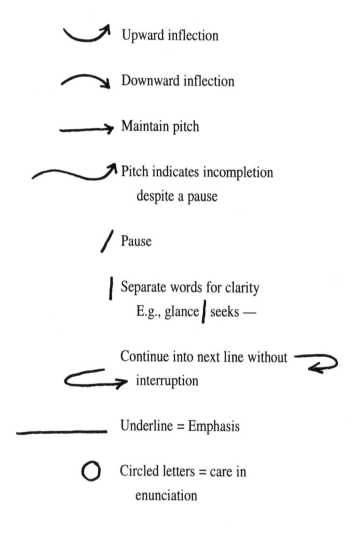

Upward inflection

Downward inflection

Maintain pitch

Pitch indicates incompletion
despite a pause

Pause

Separate words for clarity
E.g., glance | seeks —

Continue into next line without
interruption

Underline = Emphasis

Circled letters = care in
enunciation

Examples

Avoid the monotony of the "four-line syndrome" by continuing past the end of the line when feasible. (Remember the "Trees" example?) Break the monotony of four short lines whenever possible to avoid fragmentation and to keep thought-lines alive and vital.

Twenty-Fourth Sunday in Ordinary Time A (130)
Psalm 103:1–2, 3–4, 9–10, 11–12

R/. (8) The Lord is kind and merciful, slow to
anger, and rich in compassion.

Bless the LORD, O my soul;

and all my being/bless his holy name.

Bless the LORD, O my soul,

and forget not all his benefits.

R/. The Lord is kind and merciful, slow to
anger, and rich in compassion.

He pardons all your iniquities, /

heals all your ills,

He redeems your life from destruction, /

and crowns you with kindness and

compassion.

R/. The Lord is kind and merciful, slow to:
anger, and rich in compassion.

Seventh Sunday of Easter A (59)
Psalm 27:1, 4, 7–8

R/. (13) I believe that I shall see the good
things of the Lord in the land of the living.

The LORD is my light and my salvation;

whom should I fear?

The LORD is my life's refuge;

of whom should I be afraid?

R/. I believe that I shall see the good things of
   the Lord in the land of the living.

One thing I ask of the LORD;

   this I seek:

to dwell in the house of the LORD

   all the days of my life, /

that I may gaze on the loveliness of the LORD

   and contemplate his temple.

R/. I believe that I shall see the good things of
   the Lord in the land of the living.

Hear, O LORD, the sound of my call;

   have pity on me, and answer me.

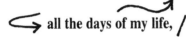

Of you my heart speaks;

   you my glance seeks.

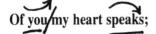

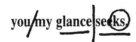

R/. I believe that I shall see the good things of
   the Lord in the land of the living.

Fifth Sunday of Easter A (52)

Psalm 33:1–2, 4–5, 18–19

R/. (22) Lord, let your mercy be on us, as we place our trust in you.

Exult, you just, in the LORD;

praise from the upright is fitting.

Give thanks to the LORD on the harp;

with the ten-stringed lyre chant his praises.

R/. Lord, let your mercy be on us, as we place our trust in you.

Upright is the word of the LORD,

and all his works are trustworthy.

He loves justice and right;

of the kindness of the LORD the earth is

full.

R/. Lord, let your mercy be on us, as we place our trust in you.

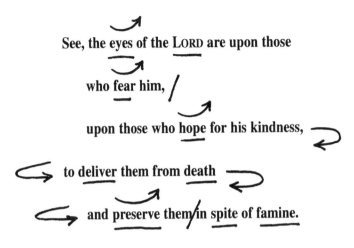

See, the eyes of the LORD are upon those

who fear him, /

upon those who hope for his kindness,

to deliver them from death

and preserve them in spite of famine.

R/. Lord, let your mercy be on us, as we place
our trust in you.

Divorce the Music!

Be very cautious of psalms that have familiar musical settings. Psalm 91 is an example. Michael Joncas
has two beautiful settings: "Be with Me, Lord" and
an adaptation of the text in "On Eagle's Wings." In
either case, mentally try not to hear the music;
ignore the melodic line, or the words will fall into
the rhythmic patterns of the song. There are many
similar examples that could be cited; the same suggestion is always applicable.

Redundancy

Repeated words and redundant phrases can easily become monotonous if inflectional patterns are repeated constantly. However, the beauty of Psalm 19 is really felt if the reader searches for ways to change the inflectional directions of the lines.

Easter Vigil ABC (41)
Psalm 19:8, 9, 10, 11
> R/. (John 6:68c) Lord, you have the words of everlasting life.

The law of the LORD is perfect, /

refreshing the soul;

the decree of the LORD is trustworthy,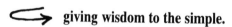

giving wisdom to the simple.

> R/. Lord, you have the words of everlasting life.

The precepts of the LORD are right, /

rejoicing the heart;

the command of the LORD is clear,

enlightening the eye.

R/. Lord, you have the words of everlasting life.

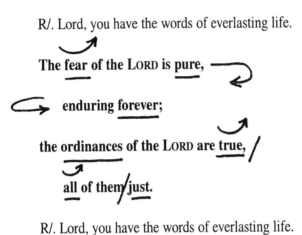

The fear of the LORD is pure,

enduring forever;

the ordinances of the LORD are true, /

all of them just.

R/. Lord, you have the words of everlasting life.

They are more precious than gold, /

than a heap of purest gold;

sweeter also than syrup

or honey from the comb.

R/. Lord, you have the words of everlasting life.

The first line will be stronger if emphasis is placed on "Lord." It also avoids the possibility of tripping over "law" of the "Lord." After that, use the changing word of the phrase for emphasis, avoiding leaning on "Lord."

Inappropriate Pauses

Hesitating with uncertainty before proper nouns is disruptive to the thought-lines in readings and psalms. When silence precedes a name that is awkward and unfamiliar, it only heightens the anticipation of the listeners to what is often a disaster. The remedy? Work on pronunciation ahead of time to be comfortable with it. The genealogy of Jesus found in Matthew 1:1–25 is never read by lectors since it is a Gospel, but is a wonderful opportunity to practice and master the pronunciation of proper names from the Hebrew Scriptures. It appears in the readings for the vigil of Christmas, all three years of the cycle. There will be a more extensive treatment of this subject in a subsequent section of this book.

Spend extra time on the psalms. Anyone who has a love for poetry and reads a great deal of it will find gauging the appropriate pausing places in the psalms much easier than people who confine themselves to prose. Granted, they are often sung by the cantor and congregation. When spoken, they must be just as meaningful as when sung, and they will be, if they are phrased effectively.

Volume

This is a very difficult topic for a book. I guess it can be summed up in one sentence: Volume must be appropriate. But just what is "appropriate"?

As with pacing, the normal volume used for everyday conversation is *not* appropriate and will not suffice. Lectors must be constantly aware that they are proclaiming the word and not merely talking.

I vividly recall a friend coming to Mass when I lectored for the first time. Afterward, she remarked that she did not recognize my voice — she "had heard me talk but never heard me speak before" and she had known me for years! There is a decided difference. The lector is indeed a public speaker, a proclaimer.

Every church has a different amplification system and a different acoustical situation. Consequently, there are no hard and fast rules applied in all places.

People often entertain the idea that amplification creates clarity. How wrong they are! Think for a moment. One tiny frame of thirty-five millimeter film can be enlarged to fill Radio City Music Hall's giant screen. However, if the film is not sharply focused at its point of origin, it becomes more blurry and diffused as it is enlarged. Without color, it might be hard to decipher what the picture is — someone's income tax form or a forest!

Sound is exactly the same. If the speaker's diction is not precise, amplification only makes it more indistinct. Just as a film, blurry at the start, becomes more unfocused with enlargement, sound does the same. The clarity of the diction itself is of prime importance.

Some lectors feel they can get very close to the microphone and let the system do all the work. That is not really effective. The system will amplify the *words* but it will not carry the strength of the message.

Singers on television — some singing very softly — appear to be biting the head off the microphone they are so close to it. Unfortunately, the untrained person seeing this imitates the situation without realizing two things: First, in a professional venue, there is always an engineer working with the singer to make all necessary adjustments, and second, professionals always employ a great deal of energy regardless of how softly they may be singing or speaking. The operative word here is *energy*. A skilled performer energizes a message with breath support, sharp enunciation, proper pacing and a genuine conviction of the text.

It is absolutely mandatory to know your system and your space, that is, you must know your church acoustically. Practice with the system turned on or you will never learn how to use it. When you practice in an empty church, you will notice reverberations which will not occur at a crowded Mass. Bodies absorb sound. In the vacant building, your voice will bounce off the empty wooden pews. But when the pews are filled with people (Oh, wouldn't that be a joy — to be filled!), the sound is not reflected. Consequently, more volume is needed at liturgies than at rehearsals.

In addition to absorbing sound, bodies also *make* sound. At the time the lector is beginning, the congregation is getting itself settled, sitting for the first time; hymnals are being replaced and people are adjusting, preparing for the liturgy of the word. A reminder: this is why the time used to open the lectionary is so useful at this point. It creates the space to discreetly allow for this commotion to end.

Often I have jokingly suggested that the Catholic Church be renamed, "The Church of Late Comers." Many times Mass begins with a sparsely filled church. Doors keep opening during the readings, the Gospel, the homily and, by Communion, the assembly has multiplied. Late arrivals create noises, regardless of how quiet everyone may try to be.

I recently learned of a church where ushers held all late comers at the doors until there was an appropriate break and an opportunity to find seating. No one is seated during the readings or Gospel; they wait and are escorted to seats at a point when a pause will not be disruptive. I do not know this parish but I would guess people would probably be more prompt than in other places, because being seated in so obvious a fashion would be embarrassing. Unfortunately this practice is not universal and, in most parishes, delayed arrivals create a need for additional volume.

Everyone should be aware of the need for higher volume in the summer. Opened windows can add all sorts of distracting noises that break the serenity of the moment. Also, the central air-conditioning systems in summer can be much noisier than the heating systems are in winter. Large fans also can distract. It is important for the lector to be aware of these differences and adjust volume accordingly. Otherwise, the comfort that cooling devices provide outweighs the purpose of the congregation's attendance — to literally *hear* Mass.

Crowding the microphone (i.e., being too close) is unwise. With some systems the sound is blurred, but in all systems imperfections in speech are amplified — neglected consonants and carelessly enunciated syllables are exaggerated. In less sophisticated systems, "p"s will pop, "s"s will hiss, etc. When lectors are too close to the microphone, the sound can be as undesirable as when they are too distant. We might liken it to putting a photograph under a microscope. Nothing is improved or changed — only enlarged, showing all flaws.

I cannot stress enough that microphones are costly and should be handled wisely and carefully. Whenever they are moved for adjustments, *handle with care;* move them slowly and gently. Never, ever, knock on a mike to determine if it is "live." During the entrance song and other introductory rites, the lector can determine whether or not the system is turned on by listening discerningly.

Microphones used in churches cannot be omnidirectional; they would pick up and amplify all the noises of the congregations. In practices, you must work with your mike to find the ideal distance from it, its live area and the adjustment that is right for you personally.

Added volume needs added breath and support. Without them, the larynx assumes the responsibility and the vocal cords strain to make the louder sound. This type of vocalization is not pleasant. It reflects the strain the cords are feeling. Volume increased by added breath is not only a more pleasant sound, but enriched and infinitely more soothing to the listeners. More importantly, it is much healthier for the speaker. Incorrect volume support over an extended period of time will cause serious vocal damage requiring medical attention.

If you return to the ambo to read the General Intercessions (provided no deacon is present), remember to readjust the height of the microphone. The priest has read the Gospel and delivered his homily from this same location. Perhaps he is more than six feet tall (as are some of the priests in my parish) and you are only five feet four inches (as I am). There is a definite need for readjustment of the mike or you will not be reaping the benefits of your amplification system and reading effectively.

Conviction of Text and Development of Inflections

Conviction of Text

Most people are clueless as to how arduous the task of producing a television commercial is. Much time and effort is spent solely on the sound. The person chosen for the commercial must not only have the desired vocal quality and clarity, but most of all, must be able to sell the product. The voice alone must convince viewers that Coca-Cola® is the absolute best of all soft drinks, that Jell-O® chocolate pudding is the only thing that belongs in your child's lunch box or that you really would "Rather have a Buick."™

The actor is just that — an actor — who must first make it real to himself and believe in the product so that it can be believable to you. If he has never tasted Coke or Jell-O and delivers the text half-heartedly, you will never be compelled to go out and purchase the products. Somehow these TV salesmen make you feel you haven't lived if you do not drink Coke or enjoyed chocolate pudding or driven a Buick.

How do actors make commercials "sell?" The next time your television or radio is on, listen to the message. Be analytical and really analyze how it is being delivered. You will hear a voice that varies in rate, speaks some phrases faster than others, varies in pitch, uses inflectional patterns to add conviction and most of all, speaks every word crisply and clearly. All these things are necessary to touch the public and to convince them to use the products.

As lectors we are very fortunate: we need not be actors; we believe in what we are proclaiming, but how often is scripture read in an unconvincing way? Probably more often than not. If you truly believe in what you are reading, then bring the word to life and do not simply read words. To do this you must understand the scriptural passages despite how obscure the meaning of the readings can be.

A young musician, singer or pianist may perform a very challenging work of Mozart or another composer. All the notes may be articulated clearly and accurately and there may be no memory lapses. But somehow the surface is never penetrated. It becomes a performance of notes, lacking depth of perception and insight into the meaning. That is why it is so astounding when a young Midori-like violinist appears on the scene, an absolute genius with a solid technique and the intellectual and emotional development so rare in anyone, particularly in one so young. She does not overwhelm an audience with phenomenal playing and dazzle them with astounding technique only, but conveys the message the composer intended.

The tremendous study and preparation any performer does to more completely understand the composer's intent is something most people would never imagine. To better interpret one aria, a singer will learn the entire opera and listen to other compositions of the same composer to better understand his style.

The lector should read the passages that precede and follow the excerpt to be used at Mass to get a fuller understanding of what the selection means. How often, if a small paragraph is taken out of a newspaper article or a speech, the message becomes unclear and ambiguous! But when the entire article is read or the full speech heard it makes perfect sense. Lectors must do their "homework" if they hope to proclaim effectively.

Yes, we believe in the Scriptures, but do we always truly understand what we are reading? Do we spend time analyzing sentences? I do not mean in a grammatical sense only (although that is also wise) but really poring over the meaning until it actually sends a message to us? I cannot say this often enough: If the sentences do not mean something to you and you do not fully comprehend what you are reading, they will never mean anything to the congregation.

Developing Inflections

A major factor in being convincing is using more vocal range and inflections. This is the commercial spokesperson's stock in trade; this is what really sells a product and makes any vocal delivery — from ordinary conversation to Shakespeare or to Scripture — come to life with vitality.

The following pages will present exercises to help develop the use of stronger emphasis and demonstrate how such emphasis can change the entire meaning by choosing to accentuate a different word. Various scenarios will be offered in an attempt to make the reader aware of how varied and many the possibilities are.

Read through each sentence; read the scenario suggested, and then reread the sentence as the drama suggests. It would be wise to use the tape recorder to do this, taking note of the tremendous variations in the same words as they reflect the different situations and emotions.

A. "Why did you do that?"

Read this line in response to each of the
following situations. Let your voice and the
entire inflectional pattern vary as you would
normally ask this question in each of these
different instances:

1. You have just finished polishing the floor
   when someone comes running across it with
   muddy shoes. With a sense of frustration
   and not a little impatience, ask the question,
   "Why did you do *that?*"

2. A beautiful and unexpected gift is handed to
   you, one you realize is extravagant and
   unnecessary. With mixed emotions of pleasure, surprise and not a little confusion, you
   ask, *"Why* did you do that?"

3. Several children are into mischief; the
   mother of one directs her question to her
   child in the group asking, "Why did *you* do
   that?"

Just think of what is involved in each of these little plots. The first and third examples need a fuller tone and a faster pace, because there is a sense of impatience and anger involved. Imagine your aggravation after spending time and effort to polish the floor only to have someone walk across it and ruin all your work. The mother, to single out her own child, leans on *you;* with a sense of annoyance, the quality would again be strong though the emphasis switches to a different word.

The second plot needs a totally different approach. In your amazement at someone's unpredicted generosity, a sincere, softer and gentler tone is needed to reflect awe for the donor's kindness — a slower pace is also wise. As you begin the question, emphasize *"why,"* not with added volume but by giving it slightly more length. Enunciate *"why"* more slowly.

The last plot is more like the first in that there is a degree of anger and annoyance involved. Therefore, the pace will again be quicker and the tone stronger, particularly leaning on *"you"* as the mother vents her impatience with her own child.

4. As an added thought before we go on, who among us has never cried to God, *"Why did you do that?"* when we have been faced with affliction or tragedy? This is the essence of sincerity as it is coming from deep within our hearts and is voiced more slowly and softly.

So we have four completely different readings of the same sentence — anger, surprise, annoyance and anguish.

Concentrating on all that is involved and picturing yourself in each of these situations, say the line out loud; better still, turn on your trusty tape recorder. Listen to yourself; think the situation through again and envision each of these situations. Reread each line, stopping between each to allow for a realization of the change in attitude. Listen again; compare both renditions.

B. "I love you!"

1. As an engagement ring is being place on his intended's finger, the prospective groom proclaims, "I *love* you." Maybe he would

like to shout it, but he says it quietly and his sincerity makes him elongate the "L" and really voice the "V," which gives the word strength and intensity. Despite the lack of volume, it has the same effect as if it were shouted.

2. "Maybe no one else in the room cares for you, but *I* love you." The *"I"* is proudly and strongly uttered.

3. In a comedic fashion, a person could question incredulously, "I love *you?"*

If the tone used is sarcastic, again, the picture changes. Three little words, but how many and varied are the ways they can be used, changing the statement with variations from light comedy to tremendous sincerity and emotion.

C. "I said that."
1. Hearing a little story that has been repeated (and slightly altered with each telling), the original speaker is amazed and asks, "I said *that?"*

2. Many people are in the room and are questioned as to who bears the responsibility for the statement just disclosed. One admits, *"I said that!"*

3. If questioned as to intent, one would say, "Make no mistake about it; I really meant it when I *said* that." The tone is strong and authoritative.

D. "I understand why you did that."
1. Several people are present. Most are doubtful but one speaks up, *"I understand why you did that."* Saying "I" strongly and with conviction shows belief in the person addressed.

2. If *"understand"* is enunciated more slowly and with a warmer quality the same situation switches, because the speaker is evincing a sense of empathy.

3. Placing the emphasis on *"you"* and speaking faster changes the meaning again — "I'm puzzled why others are involved, but I

can grasp why *you* are involved." This is your feeling and reaction.

4. The same tempo, changing the strength to *"that"* means the speaker cannot figure out why the person might do something else but can comprehend *this* situation.

E. "I can't believe she won a Tony."

1. A Tony is the epitome of achievement for all Broadway performers, directors, etc. Many other awards are offered for theater but none is quite so prestigious in the United States. Therefore, to single out the magnitude of this accomplishment, the speaker is somewhat awed as *"Tony"* is pronounced slowly with a sense close to reverence (particularly if it is uttered by an aspiring actor).

2. Totally incredulous among the theater-going public, slowing the enunciation of *"can't"* strengthens the almost impossible idea that the winner was a complete surprise.

3. Another nominee, in reacting to the announcement of the winner, has more than a touch of anger and envy in her voice as she says the sentence rather quickly, leaning on and delaying the pronoun, *"she,"* showing her bitterness.

4. A true friend of the winner responds with much sincerity and genuine enthusiasm. The person speaks slowly with much warmth in the voice and, using the consonants very strongly (especially the "V") in *"believe"* shows obvious pride in the winner. You can literally hear the smile in his voice.

F. "I'm sorry."
There are literally dozens of ways this can be uttered, from the innocence of a child, caught with his hand in the cookie jar, to the final words at the conclusion of a relationship. Imagine as many different situations as you can and respond appropriately, changing tempo, quality and pitch each time.

Some passages needing special care are those that begin, "O God" or "God."

If the tone and inflection are not correct, the results can be disastrous. "O God" can vary from sounding as if the speaker is taking God's name in vain to bordering on the comedic. Remember, this is direct address; you are speaking directly to God when you say, "O God, in your great love, answer me."

There are many other passages and excerpts from Scripture that need special attention. These will be discussed in a subsequent section of this book.

We might define the inflections in speech as the music of the language. Even if the vocabulary is incomprehensible, one can easily hear the difference in the "melody" of Swedish or Spanish or Russian or German or English. Even "American English" varies in tempo and tune in different parts of this vast country of ours. Every language has its own "tune," pattern and rhythm. This is the important aspect of a language — its music.

Devoid of these "melodies," speech is flat and totally uninteresting. People born with a hearing deficiency, who have learned to speak with the aid of a therapist, minus the benefit of hearing the music of the language, speak in a monotone, without any inflections. This type of flat speech shows the reality of the value of tonal differences.

When lay*men* first became lectors after Vatican II, they tended to read in a very monotonal fashion, due in no small measure to the fact that they had grown up listening to the priests saying Mass in Latin and felt they were being dramatic and "hammy" if they employed any variation in pitch. The men "blazed the trail," so to speak. When the ladies followed a few years later, they were more attuned to a modulated sound. Also, the women were more accustomed to reading stories to their little ones. "I'll huff and I'll puff 'til I blow the house down" was always dramatically read. They seemed to find it easier because they employed more pitch modifications and pace changes to make their tales to their children more exciting and meaningful. Consequently, women were less self-conscious in using a more melodic proclamation.

Speech devoid of color, pitch and pace changes is quite dull and monotonous. More lectors tend to "walk on the dull side," making the reading flat and uninteresting, than those who tread on the over-emotional side. This is when the tape recorder is invaluable. Practicing with it, listening discerningly and thoughtfully experimenting with inflections can only help to make a lector more effective.

How to Practice

If you are a doctor, pianist, dancer, golfer or whatever, friends constantly shower you with little objects of jewelry, tee-shirts, even anecdotes pertaining to your chosen profession. They even collect jokes for you. Several times I've been told the one about the tenor who sang *"Che gelida canina"* instead of *"Che gelida manina."* The first-act aria in *La Bohème* has Rodolfo singing of the coldness of Mimi's hand *(manina)* and certainly not about her dog *(canina)*. That story sort of fits midway between my being a musician and a reader, dealing with diction in both vocal arts and liturgical ministries.

Some time ago, a friend sent me an article with this story. I paraphrase:

A company of actors was touring in Ireland; the leading performer was someone of the caliber of a Richard Chamberlain. The troupe arrived in a small village and the leading man visited the local church. He spoke with the pastor and asked if he might have the privilege of lectoring at Mass on the weekend. The priest was delighted to have someone so famous read for Mass. Early Saturday morning, the actor presented himself at the rectory. Thinking this famous person was confused, the pastor hastened to inform him: "Mass is tomorrow, Sunday, not today." "Yes, Father, I know," the actor replied, "But I've come to borrow the lectionary so that I might practice."

Does that not give a message to us all? The professional person with training and experience can recognize the need to practice and prepare. How unfortunate that people sometimes think anyone can read and, in consequence, the same people consider themselves as lectors above the need for practice!

Each of us was given a unique and special gift by God. We have each been endowed with a voice — granted, some are better than others, but nonetheless, a voice. How few of us have ever done anything about it! We come equipped with this; God gave it to us; we did not have to purchase it. Do we really value it? Have we ever done anything to learn to understand its mechanism or try to improve it? Unfortunately, as with most things we receive without cost, we do not always value it as we ought. We think, "Everyone can speak. Everyone can read." and little or no effort is made to improve.

Some of us who can afford it, purchase a piano or another instrument. When we do, we expect to spend time and invest money and effort in learning to play this expensive piece of furniture. Otherwise, it is just that — a piece of furniture. If we have some ability and are able to read music or even play by ear, we usually seek a teacher to help us have greater understanding and control, and, consequently, derive more pleasure from it. We expect to study and practice to improve.

What happens in a lectoring practice session? This changes drastically from parish to parish. In my private teaching, I spend much time guiding and directing new students in the way to practice and I think a few suggestions for lectors are in order here.

When do you begin to practice? Preparation for reading the Scriptures must not be a last-minute thing. I have worked with lectors in my own parish for many years and the sessions have always been on Monday nights. Why Monday? Not because of the availability of the church, but rather to give them the greatest amount of time before Sunday to digest and implement ideas. They have the opportunity to think about what we have discussed and corrected and have ample chance to thoroughly digest it.

Often someone has told me that at first the reading was a total loss to her; then after we worked on it, discussed it, etc., the words formed phrases she could hear, and consequently, the message became obvious. Some have said that they take the readings while traveling to work and study them en route; some keep them at their bedsides. Whenever they do it and wherever they do it, they refer to it during the week. By the weekend, they are comfortable with the readings, which makes for a more successful proclamation of the Scriptures.

Let us first assume there is no one to supervise the practice and the lector is left to her or his own devices. Almost every parish has some type of paperback booklet containing the readings. Try to get your own copy to use for practicing. If you own a lectionary, photocopy the pages to avoid marking your book. Your interpretation may change three years hence when these readings are used again. Use the copy for study and practice. Read and reread the passage. Underline words that need emphasis and put slashes between words where it is appropriate to breathe. Remember, if it is not making sense to you, it cannot make sense to anyone else.

Examples for Practice

The following excerpts from the lectionary indicate a method of preparation which I have found to be extremely valuable. Interpretation can and should vary from person to person and from one day to the next. However, these are examples of how to practice and to find more meaning in the Scripture. As you ponder over sentence structure and so on you will find the inner meaning ringing clearer.

Twenty-Second Sunday in Ordinary Time C (126)
Sirach 3:17–18, 20, 28–29

A reading from the Book of Sirach

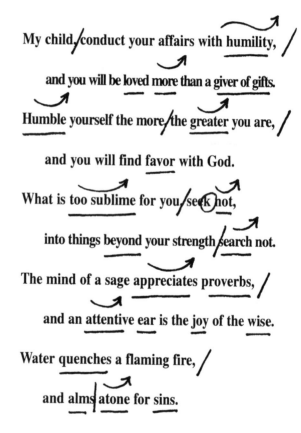

My child, conduct your affairs with humility, /

and you will be loved more than a giver of gifts.

Humble yourself the more the greater you are, /

and you will find favor with God.

What is too sublime for you seek not,

into things beyond your strength search not.

The mind of a sage appreciates proverbs, /

and an attentive ear is the joy of the wise.

Water quenches a flaming fire, /

and alms atone for sins.

The word of the Lord.

Read through the entire passage first. Then, with pencil in hand, reread it deciding where emphasis should be placed and where pauses are appropriate, and mark accordingly.

Notice how accented words vary and inflectional patterns are not repeated in successive lines to avoid monotonous phrasing.

At the conclusion of all readings, pause before adding, "The word of the Lord." It is *not* the last sentence of the passage, and it demands to be separated.

The Baptism of the Lord B (Optional) (21)
Isaiah 55:1–11

A reading from the Book of the Prophet Isaiah

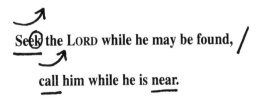

Seek the LORD while he may be found, /

    call him while he is near.

Let the scoundrel forsake his way,

    and the wicked man his thoughts;

let him turn to the LORD for mercy;

to our God, who is generous in forgiving.

For my thoughts are not your thoughts, /

nor are your ways my ways, says the LORD.

As high as the heavens are above the earth /

so high are my ways above your ways /

and my thoughts above your thoughts.

For just as from the heavens

the rain and snow come down /

and do not return there

till they have watered the earth,

making it fertile and fruitful, /

giving seed to the one who sows

and bread to the one who eats, /

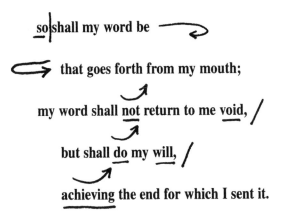

so shall my word be

that goes forth from my mouth;

my word shall not return to me void, /

but shall do my will, /

achieving the end for which I sent it.

This is an excerpt of the reading from Isaiah found in different Masses throughout the year.

The initial word, "seek" must have a strong "k," otherwise it reaches the congregation as "see the Lord," which is very different.

The repetitive pronouns in the second section need special care, as indicated.

In the final section, lines need to be more continuous, as indicated. This does not suggest quickening the pace — rather, avoid fragmenting ideas and disturbing the message.

Third Sunday of Advent B (8)

1 Thessalonians 5:16–24

A reading from the first Letter of Saint Paul

to the Thessalonians

Brothers and sisters: ⎯⎯⎯⎯

Rejoice always. Pray/without ceasing.

In all circumstances/give thanks, /

for this is the will of God for you in

Christ Jesus.

Do not quench the Spirit.

Do not despise prophetic utterances.

Test everything; retain what is good.

Refrain from every kind of evil.

This is another example of changing the position of emphasis to create a more interesting and meaningful proclamation.

106

Twenty-Eighth Sunday in Ordinary Time C (144)

2 Timothy 2:8–13

A reading from the second Letter of Saint

Paul to Timothy

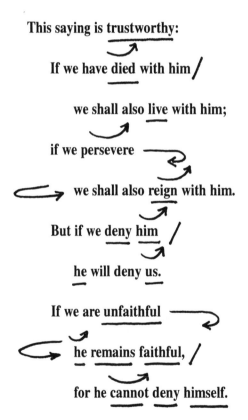

This saying is trustworthy:

If we have died with him /

     we shall also live with him;

   if we persevere

    we shall also reign with him.

But if we deny him /

    he will deny us.

If we are unfaithful

   he remains faithful, /

    for he cannot deny himself.

The above is only the second half of this passage.

The phrases are very short but must not be hurried. In fact, these are powerful ideas that lose their impact if they are not delivered more slowly and emphatically.

Second Sunday of Lent A (25)
2 Timothy 1:8b–10

A reading from the second Letter of Saint Paul to Timothy

Beloved:

Bear your share of hardship for the gospel with the strength that comes from God.

He saved us/and called us to a holy life, /
not according to our works /
but according to his own design
and the grace bestowed on us in Christ
Jesus/before time began, /

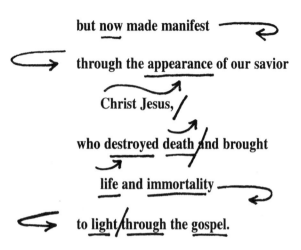

but now made manifest

through the appearance of our savior

Christ Jesus,

who destroyed death and brought

life and immortality

to light through the gospel.

After the introductory sentence, the entire passage is one sentence and only one complete idea. The vocal pattern, therefore, must suggest continuity and, though unhurried, must reflect the needed fluidity — not restful until the last word is reached.

The Holy Family of Jesus, Mary and Joseph B (17)
Hebrews 11:8, 11–12, 17–19

A reading from the Letter to the Hebrews

Brothers and sisters: ———

By faith Abraham obeyed when he was

called to go out to a place

that he was to receive as an inheritance;

he went out not knowing where he was

to go.

By faith he received power to generate,

even though he was past the normal age

(— and Sarah herself was sterile —)

for he thought that the one who had

made the promise was trustworthy.

So it was that there came forth from one man,

(himself as good as dead,)

descendants as numerous as the stars

in the sky

and as countless as the sands on the

seashore.

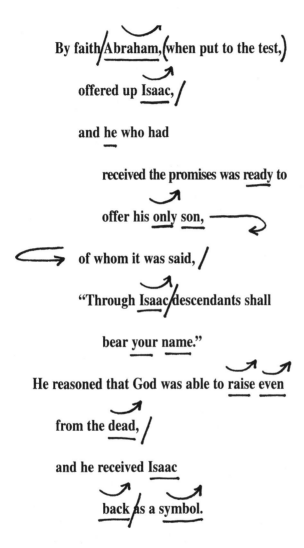

By faith Abraham, (when put to the test,)

offered up Isaac, /

and he who had

received the promises was ready to

offer his only son,

of whom it was said, /

"Through Isaac descendants shall

bear your name."

He reasoned that God was able to raise even

from the dead, /

and he received Isaac

back as a symbol.

There are occasions in the Scripture when fluency is interrupted. The above passage is an example of this. Your thought-line must go beyond that interruption; otherwise it will be just that — an interruption, and the message will dissipate. For example, "By faith Abraham (when put to the test) offered up Isaac." If you ignore "when put to the test," you hear the message of the phrase — "By faith Abraham offered up Isaac." You cannot omit any words, but you must listen beyond the parenthesis to hear where the principal idea is going and, with that in mind, read the entire sentence.

Palm Sunday of the Lord's Passion ABC (38)
Philippians 2:6–11

A reading from the Letter of Saint Paul to

the Philippians

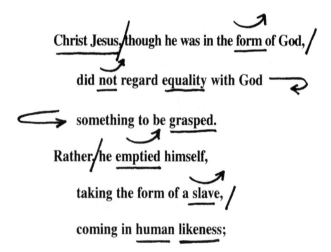

Christ Jesus, though he was in the form of God, /

did not regard equality with God

something to be grasped.

Rather, he emptied himself,

taking the form of a slave, /

coming in human likeness;

and found human in appearance,

he humbled himself, /

becoming obedient to the point of death, /

even death on a cross.

Because of this, God greatly exalted him /

and bestowed on him the name

which is above every name, /

that at the name of Jesus

every knee should bend, /

of those in heaven and on earth and

under the earth, /

and every tongue confess that

Jesus Christ is Lord, /

to the glory of God the Father.

Every Palm Sunday of the Lord's Passion, we
read this beautiful passage of Saint Paul. Carry
phrases into the next line. Remember, this does not

mean increasing the tempo, rather, the opposite is true. Though phrases are short, they are very powerful and demand to be verbalized more deliberately. Note the contrasting prepositions "in heaven and *on* earth and *under* the earth." Only in such situations as this should prepositions be accentuated.

For background information on the readings, if no priest is available to give an exegesis, several books are available that give biblical commentary. There are also various dictionaries that provide proper pronunciations of names of persons and places that may be unfamiliar.

Experienced lectors have a great advantage, if they only realize it. But occasionally it works in reverse. Sometimes familiarity breeds complacency and that is dangerous. Why do some lectors feel that because they have read that passage before no preparation is needed?

Would you be content to spend a small fortune for a ticket to hear someone on Luciano Pavarotti's level perform, if you knew he had not touched the score in three years? Or perhaps you play piano. Imagine that three years ago you learned a Beethoven Sonata. One evening you are entertaining company. Would you attempt to play it "cold," without having practiced or restudied it first? I think not! The better pianist you are, the less inclined you would be to try to play anything that has been laid to rest for three years. Yet some lectors do! Often they open the book, realize that they have read the passage previously and close the book, feeling no further refreshing or study is necessary.

As said before, familiarity is dangerous. Regardless of whether it is a sonata, a hymn, an aria or a scriptural passage, it is always a whole new experience to restudy something — to search for a deeper, fresher approach. If you are doing your job correctly, you will always be amazed when a new thought occurs to you and wonder why you did not see that before. If that does not happen, you have not searched as thoroughly as you ought. It is such a rewarding feeling when the newness does happen. The more often you read a passage, the more there is to be found in it.

Using Tape Recorders

Tape recorders are very common and inexpensive in today's world. They can be valuable tools for lectors practicing the Scriptures, but they must be used judiciously.

When we listen to professional recordings we hear magnificent sound. That high quality would have been deemed impossible years ago. It is possible for someone with a small voice to sound tremendous in recordings (and I do not mean small in the sense of volume only). The engineers and the equipment available today can perform miracles. Wrong notes and other undesirable qualities can be corrected or altered. Almost nothing is impossible. All this produces a recording that, unlike live performance, is just about perfect. The sterility of it is unnatural, because in actual performance, the human element enters in and things do go wrong. We are spoiled and have become accustomed to hearing beautifully recorded sound through excellent stereo systems.

The small tape recorder you may use cannot possibly reproduce sound accurately. Imagine the cost of producing a professional recording: the fees for the artists, the studio rental, the equipment, the time for "take" after "take" until the performers and producers are satisfied, etc. Even one microphone would cost several times more than a case of little recorders. So how can you hope to reproduce your voice accurately? You cannot.

The reason I have seemingly digressed is to emphasize the difference between a professional and an amateur recording. I have been seated with lectors hearing themselves for the first time on tape, arguing with me, "That is not my voice. I do not sound like that." Even more exasperating is the comment, "If I sound like that, I'll never lector again!" Tape recorders can be valuable tools but only if they are used constructively. Record someone else whose voice is familiar to you; listen and compare mentally what that person sounds like in actuality and then on the tape. Realize that same difference occurs with your voice.

Regardless, these small recorders are helpful. They enable you to check your inflectional patterns, your pacing, your pronunciation and enunciation — or lack thereof.

If you are practicing at home, do not sit with the recorder at your side and talk into it as if you were on the telephone. This will be of no avail. Place it at the opposite end of the room and project your voice as if you were in church. The ideal place to use it is in church where it can be set in a pew at a greater distance and give a truer sense of projection. If it is placed too close, a conversational tone will be used, opposite that needed to proclaim the Scripture.

No new lector should ever be assigned without first having had the opportunity to practice reading in church: to stand at the microphone at the ambo and get the feel of the atmosphere. There is a need to accustom oneself to the sound of the voice in this location. Use your tape recorder here.

Being Observant

In today's world, we have the opportunity to enjoy the best performers in our homes every day. We can observe fine newscasters or actors of all sorts twenty-four hours of the day, should we choose. Television and radio puts the very best at our disposal should we want to emulate these people. Granted, everyone in the public eye is not the epitome of perfection and someone to be imitated. Some have come to great prominence despite, or maybe because of, a slight lisp or a faulty "L"; it becomes a type of trademark. But it still is a fault and not to be copied. Often we feel it must be right if it is being done by the media and the person involved is highly paid. Wrong is still wrong, regardless of who is involved or what the salary may be.

Newscasters are very different from actors; actors are portraying a role and must absorb the character, traits and characteristics of the person they are portraying. Newscasters project themselves. We could even say they are "proclaiming" the day's important happenings to us. Therefore, they are doing something closer to what we do as lectors. Notice how they vary the pace and the pitch in the deliverance of the news. Copy is not read flat and devoid of all the devices that actors use, but these devices are used in moderation and fit within the reporter's own personality, without assuming another character. Those who "proclaim" the news to us are good examples to lectors, insofar as delivery of the text is concerned.

One of the most valuable aspects of television and radio is the opportunity to develop a sense of discernment — to learn to be wisely critical. It is so often easy to be critical. Many of us are very quick to be harsh in appraising someone else's work. I have always felt that professionals with years of training and experience are much less judgmental and more appreciative of other's efforts because they understand all that performing entails. Criticism does not always mean being derogatory. There is a positive side too, and much can be said in praise.

Critique

In many parishes, too little time is spent preparing lectors. A choir is always expected to rehearse, and cantors also, do not attempt to lead the song without practice. In many cases, cantors have professional training. In contrast, lectors are often left to their own devices to practice and prepare the readings, which amazes me.

Lectors have a dual dilemma. Not only do they need instruction and training in delivery but they also need some help with the exegesis — someone to give them a sense of the meaning of the text. Again, if it is not understandable and meaningful to the lector, it cannot touch someone else. I am well aware of the shortage of priests today and how heavily burdened they are. Even so, somehow time should be made to help lectors or potential lectors. The effort and hours spent nurturing these ministers of the word can only bear fruit abundantly.

In many parishes, large amounts of money are spent on elaborate amplification systems. I do not mean to imply that this is unnecessary. Quite the contrary; but if care is not taken and lectors are not shown the proper use of the system, the delivery of the text will not convey as it should.

In some parishes, the lectors meet in the church and read for each other as a peer review. This, to me, is the least favorable of all methods. Personalities and egos come into play and often more harm than good is done; it is simply counter-productive. Often, one person elects him/herself to critique the others when there is actually no background to validate the criticisms. Such people can be rather officious and domineering and have disastrous effects on more timid individuals.

Those who work with lectors must be careful with their critiques. Insincere flattery is dangerous and ineffective. Praise is necessary and appreciated when it is merited. If praise is given undeservedly, when it *is* merited it will not be valued. When I was a teenager, a voice teacher with whom I studied was constantly complimenting me. Young as I was, I knew certain things were not yet right despite her glowing words. I remember wondering how would I know when she really had need to praise me. Most people sense the undeserved compliments and do not accept or value them. There are always some who will gratefully receive these plaudits and feel they have no further need to improve. This is why criticism can be dangerous and must be treated carefully.

Praise when it is merited! It is appreciated and can be a source of encouragement and inspiration. Novice and veteran lectors alike are grateful for a word of praise when it is deserved. I guess you get the opinion that I am definitely not a fan of unsupervised practice.

It is irrelevant whether the setting is a tiny church on a weekday in cold and snowy February or a huge cathedral on a beautifully sunny Easter morning, the readings are still "The word of the Lord." And the readings deserve the same preparation so that they may be proclaimed properly and effectively.

Making Mistakes and Dealing with Them

Preparation certainly helps us avoid them, but as humans we do make mistakes at times, regardless of how well prepared we may be.

I will always remember the first time I read for the Easter Vigil. I was still an oddity, a woman near the altar as a lector, which was a cause for added tension. The first reading that evening was the mandatory story of the deliverance of the Jews, Exodus 14:15 — 15:1. As I was reading, I was aware that something was not right but I could not catch it. How many times does the name "Israelite" occur in that passage? Six times, to be exact. I was consistent (though incorrect) — each time it appeared, I said, "Israelis," updating the name thousands of years. After Mass, when we returned to the sacristy, the moderator of the lectors approached me and inquired, "What were you doing — a commercial for El Al Airlines?"

On one occasion, I heard someone read, "They came bearing gold, myrrhincense, and frank." When I questioned him afterward, he repeated it exactly the same way but with a more defensive quality in his voice. Until I asked "Frank who?" he did not realize the mistake. We all had a good laugh about it. From then on, he always enunciated with the greatest care — *frank*incense.

If you read "Jesus Christ" instead of "Christ Jesus," let it go; it is unimportant. If, however, you speak of the *immorality* of God rather than his *immortality,* I would suggest you correct yourself immediately. Seriously, in any case, realize that mistakes can and do happen; that is reality! If something goes wrong, do not acknowledge it in any way, with a smile, giggle, embarrassed glance or any sort of gesture. More often than not, a slight error will pass unnoticed by the assembly members. If you do anything that calls attention to it, you upset yourself as well as alerting everyone that something went awry.

One big difference between the professional and the amateur is the way mistakes are handled. The inexperienced person who has a little problem becomes flustered and allows it to continue to bother him as he goes ahead, thereby setting himself up for further difficulties.

The professional, if he encounters any problem, redeems himself quickly by dismissing all thoughts of the error and concentrates all the more intensely on where he is at and where he is going. Otherwise, the entire performance suffers. What is done is over and cannot be changed in any form of "live performance," but if you choose, you can forget what occurred and focus instead on what is yet to come.

To sum up the difference between a professional and an amateur in one phrase, I would say, "a sense of responsibility." That responsibility demands preparedness. The last ten minutes or so prior to an orchestral concert are always a source of pleasure to me. The members of the orchestra begin assembling on stage and practicing difficult or troublesome passages; the instrumentalists are concentrating so acutely that they are completely oblivious to the sounds and to the people around them. That cacophony is to me a delight to witness. These sections being practiced by extraordinary musicians (and believe me, in an orchestra such as the New York Philharmonic, they *are* extraordinary) are passages they have been performing over and over, yet they refuse to expect them to "happen" automatically. They want just one more chance to practice. The responsibility that the professional feels to the composer, to the conductor, to fellow performers and to himself is something which escapes the average listener.

Regardless of how often a particular passage may have been read, the lector should not take anything for granted or fall into a sense of complacency. This is the breeding ground for mistakes and disastrous proclamations. Professionals are never satisfied. "Good enough" is a non-existent term; it can always be better and they strive to that end.

If a lector has the opportunity to read a passage a few consecutive years (those readings which occur in all three years of the cycle), it should afford the chance to reexamine the reading, search more deeply into its meaning, make it touch new depths within and provide new ideas to be projected. If a lector feels a sense of complacency and finds no need to restudy the passage because it is familiar, this creates the opportunity for all sorts of mistakes plus a very dull and uninspiring proclamation of the scripture — one that is totally ineffective.

Nerves and Their Control

A famous performer once remarked, "Anyone who says he is never nervous is either a fool or a liar." Strong language, indeed, but I must say I heartily agree.

When I first began performing as a pre-schooler, I did not understand the meaning of the word "nerves." However, I have very vivid recollections of my mother in the control room, mouthing the words with me and looking very anxious. At the time, I did not understand her actions or anxiety. Young children are blissfully ignorant of what it means to be nervous. They are taught and rehearsed in what they do; the moment arrives, they walk on stage or before the cameras and just "do their thing." Ah, the innocence of youth! If only we could bottle it and market it!

In my own personal experience and in subsequent years through my teaching, I have sensed the manifestation of nerves as the years progressed. All of a sudden, the child realizes being "cute" is not the purpose. One must have the talent, and that talent sufficiently polished, to be able to reach and touch an audience, whether through music, dance or drama. The audience has a right to expect a performance, and at some age, a child begins to be aware this right and, consequently, nerves develop. Instead of using the word "nerves," perhaps we might refer to it as an awareness of the responsibility placed on a performer. I prefer that definition, because it is a reality and truth.

The anxiety one feels in any performance situation must be controlled. That is the operative word here: control.

Years ago the Holy Father celebrated Mass at Yankee Stadium. For personal reasons, I declined a ticket and watched on television, with an infinitely better view. That celebrated lady of the American theater, recognized and admired world-wide, Helen Hayes, was one of the lectors. Television viewing leaves nothing to the imagination; the cameras are merciless. Miss Hayes was escorted to the ambo, and as she began, one could detect her anxieties. This woman, winner of all types of theatrical awards and beloved all over the world, was obviously touched by what she was about to do. Not even Shakespeare held fears for her, but proclaiming God's word was quite another matter. Despite having received two Oscars, two Tonys, an Emmy and a Grammy, this phenomenally gifted lady later remarked that this Mass "crowned every endeavor of my life."

Being nervous is nothing to be ashamed of — it's normal. But how do you manage it? How do you control it? Preparation and technique. In the lector's case, knowing how to use the vocal mechanism, knowing how to use the amplification system and understanding the text fully.

Imagine being a relatively inexperienced driver encountering a storm while operating a car with faulty brakes. Wouldn't you be nervous? Anyone with common sense would be. If you are unsure of yourself, your instrument, its control or its operation, you have every reason to have an attack of nerves, even bordering on panic. Sometimes things cannot be controlled, but if you have a dependable technique, you do have something you can rely on. When you have a first-rate car operating beautifully, you can deal with problems on the road because you can rely on the car.

There are "good nerves." These are the ones that spur us on to do what we would not believe we are capable of. These are the ones that are kept in check and not allowed to rule our minds and bodies or interfere with performances. "Good nerves" are only possible in people who have studied hard and prepared enough to be able to be in control of the situation. Otherwise, the nerves take over and everything falls apart.

Yes, there are some people who claim they are never nervous. When a pupil complains to me, "I was so nervous at the audition," my reaction is always the same: "If you weren't nervous, *I'd* be very nervous for you!" Lectors must be aware of the responsibility of touching the assembly with God's word and be as prepared and ready as possible. Then when the moment comes, they can be confident in themselves and what they are about to do.

There is an enormous difference between self-confidence and conceit. The confident person is aware of his or her abilities as well as shortcomings, and works to develop and overcome the aspects that are lacking. Knowing the road you are traveling and having an awareness of its potholes can prevent accidents en route.

The egotistical individual has an exaggerated sense of his or her talents and feels nothing is in need of improvement. This kind of person drives along the road unconscious of the possible pitfalls and, with a sense of over-confidence, can easily have an accident or a mishap.

We have all had the experience of meeting someone who claims never to be nervous. After reading all this, I think you will agree with me and our very knowledgeable speaker — some who claim never to sense anxiety are not being truthful. Didn't you meet people in school who claimed to have achieved straight "A's" without ever opening a book, though you knew their heads were buried in the texts all night long? The same applies here. There are also some who "do not have a nerve in their bodies." But are they really worth listening to?

Just as we have "good cholesterol," which works in our blood on "bad cholesterol," we have good nerves in our system which spur us on, but only after they have done their job on the "bad nerves" by controlling them during performances.

It really doesn't matter how you feel before or after a performance — only how you feel *during* a performance. If your concentration is as focused as it should be and one hundred percent of your thoughts are directed toward the job at hand, there is no place for nerves. If you are totally engrossed in the deliverance of the text, you haven't time to think about being anxious.

From early childhood to the present, I have never and will never attempt to do anything without God's assistance. I have stood backstage as house lights were lowered and the din of the audience diminished to a hushed anticipation (and believe me, that's a scary moment — one which tempts you to turn and run away) and in front of non-Catholic conductors and accompanists, I have always made the Sign of the Cross and reminded God that he provided me with this opportunity to use the gifts he gave me. I have done my best to develop them and prepare for this occasion. Now it's all up to him and I am secure in his hands.

When the day comes (and I pray it never will) that I feel I can do it on my own and I don't have that tinge inside — I prefer to call it a respect for the awesome responsibility of proclaiming the Scripture — I will retire as a lector and never read again. If it is not meaningful enough to evoke a response in me, it will never be meaningful to a congregation. When reading lacks meaning it is irresponsible; when it has meaning it is effective.

Frequently Fractured Phrases and Woefully Wounded Words

"Why can't the English learn how to speak?" asked Henry Higgins through the lyricist Alan Jay Lerner in "My Fair Lady."

Indeed, why can't *Americans* learn how to speak and take pride in their native tongue? How often we hear people remark on the beauty of other languages! We may think French has such a romantic sound, and Italian, so sensuous. There is nothing lacking in our native tongue except in the way we use it.

Singers also are guilty when they claim how much they enjoy singing in foreign languages and how much easier it is to enunciate. I dispute that. Having sung in many languages, I don't find it to be true. Singing or speaking in a tongue other than one's primary tongue requires more care in pronunciation and enunciation, and often, in both song and speech, the added care allows for clearer diction. In our native English, the diphthongs often create difficulties in song, but with the aid of a competent teacher and practice, these problems can be mastered.

Recently, I was privileged to attend a performance of the New York Philharmonic when Christopher Plummer made music along with the orchestra without singing a note. The score was composed by William Walton for the film "Henry V," produced and directed by Sir Laurence Olivier. This performance, an arrangement by Christopher Palmer, was performed by the orchestra, with the narration undertaken by the superb Mr. Plummer.

The Philharmonic is at a peak; as described by its musical director, Kurt Mazur, they are, "One hundred and seven virtuosi who choose to play together," and their sound is phenomenal!

On this occasion, they were magnificently matched by the marvelous actor, who made the English language magically musical. It was a joy that night to hear my native tongue so beautifully treated. Any language can be lush, vibrant and exciting, provided it is spoken properly. The point is to take pride in the language you use to proclaim the word.

English comes in many varieties with a tremendous amount of regional differences. Bostonians differ from Chicagoans, Texans from Virginians and Brooklynites from San Franciscans. Added to this regional variety are the accents of new citizens.

But what never ceases to amaze me is the variety within a relatively short distance. The mileage is not that extensive but the color of speech changes greatly between Boston and New York or Philadelphia and Washington, etc. One could spend pages discussing the differences that indicate a person's home city, but I am not trying to completely remake anyone. Lectors should not try to remove all regionalisms as if they were auditioning for a network anchor position. Solve at least the glaring problems and fix the bad habits, such as slurred or careless pronunciations, and attempt to make your speech the best possible in your locality.

There are some words which are dreadfully maligned or carelessly enunciated. Often, we become so accustomed to their sound that a correct pronunciation seems wrong. It is not surprising that it is difficult to adapt to a new way of saying something.

Most of the following words appear in the Scripture passages; others may be found in the General Intercessions. These are all words which are frequently "fractured." Quite honestly, most have been heard by priest celebrants during Mass.

Some of the mispronunciations cause a phrase to be ludicrous, sometimes bizarre, sometimes confusing, but always distracting. Most times it happens because the reader has not consulted a dictionary, a more knowledgeable lector or the celebrant. If there is any doubt in your mind, ask someone or check a dictionary. Humble pie is more easily digested than crow! Do not be embarrassed to request help with pronunciation — particularly with proper nouns.

For proper nouns, every lector should have access to a pronunciation guide. There are several on the market, obtainable from a religious article and book store. Recently, I heard something sounding vaguely like "lettuce." It should have been Leviticus. Sometimes, inadequately prepared lectors see combinations of letters and in their anxiety (caused by a lack of preparedness) misread the noun in a fashion that is totally inexplicable.

"Paul to the Filipinos" and "Paul to the Philippines" are very common mistakes and have been told to me several times. Wait! It gets better! Priests in various parts of the country have given me examples such as "Paul to the Colostomies," and "Paul to the Fallopians." Poor Saint Paul! Recently, Caesarea became "Caesarean" and Joseph of Arimathea, Joseph of *"arrhythmia."* Why all these medical associations? Unpreparedness, coupled with hastily seeing a group of letters similar to a familiar (though totally inappropriate and irrelevant) word, created this woeful situation. Somehow, Nebuchadnezzer and Abednego seem to have a better chance at accuracy.

Frequently Fractured Phrases

Abram
This is not a misprint; refer to Thursday of the Fifth week of Lent (Genesis 17:3–9); God changed Abram's name to Abraham.

Book of Exodus
Pronounce "ex" — not eggs.

Christ's/peace
Slowly enunciate "sts" and slightly separate words.

St. Paul to the Colossians
Do not say "galoshes."

Holy Spirit
Use a short "i" — not *spear*-it.

human being	Use two syllables "be-ing" — not *bean.*
in/inapproachable light	Separate words carefully, use five syllables for in' a pro' cha ble.
in/sincere	Separate and emphasize "sincere" or it becomes "insincere," reversing the meaning.
Jesus' name	Do not add extra "s" — not Jesuses.
Joses	This is not a misprint for Joseph.
judges/justly	Separate and emphasize "justly" to avoid blurring the words together.
Niger	Pronounce carefully to avoid an ethnic slur.

protects/strangers	Separate words, carefully enunciating "cts" — not "proteks."
racial reconciliation	Slowly and clearly enunciate each syllable.
see what *love* **the Father has**	Love is the focus of the phrase; use "l" strongly; let the teeth voice "v" by connecting with the lower lip; this strengthens the sound and meaning; "luf" is meaningless.
seek **the Lord**	Enunciate the "k," *seeing* the Lord is very different from *seeking* him.
sewed *loincloths* **together**	Never *lion*cloths or even loin*claws!*

the *kindness*
of the Lord   Strong initial "k" and do
not omit the "d," a beauti-
ful and meaningful word
when spoken properly.

the *law* of the Lord   It is not "lore," no "r" —
precepts, not stories!

the *statutes*
of the Lord   Enunciate all "t's"; they
are not statues.

wanton revelry   Stress the first syllable in
"wanton," no soup;
remember to pronounce
the second "r" in revelry,
no bugle call.

whole *world*   Use final "d "to avoid
"whirl."

Woefully Wounded Words

a (as in "a reading") This article is very rarely pronounced "ay." That pronunciation is used only for exceptional emphasis; otherwise, use "uh."

the This article is said "thee" before a vowel (thee eagle) and for emphasis; otherwise "thuh."

accept vs. except Carefully pronounce "ac" or "ex" to avoid confusing the two.

all Not "awl"

always, already, etc. Use "l" clearly.

awe vs. or
blas' phemy (noun) vs.
blas pheme' (verb) Put the stress in the correct place.

both	Use "th" — tongue between the teeth.
bow	Refers to a rainbow, not a curtsy
buffets	Use "t" — not buffays (not furniture)
Calvary vs. cavalry	
catholic	Use three syllables — not "cathlic."
cease vs. seize	Careful of the "s" and "z"
child	Use one syllable — not chi-uld.
Christ's, costs, rests, tests, etc.	Use all consonants, "sts."
clothes	Use "th" — clothes, not close.

comfortable	Use four syllables.
constancy vs. consistency	
couldn't	Use "d" — not "coon't"
covenant vs. convent	
de*bau*'chery	"De *ba'* che ry," stressed syllable rhymes with "paw"
deluge	*"Del'* uge — not de *luge'*
deteriorate	Use five syllables.
diadem	*"Di'* a dem
didn't	Use "d" — not "din't."
draw vs. drawer	
endure, entrust	Use "en" — not "indoor" or "intrust."

enmity	Do not invert "n" and "m."
en' velope (noun) vs. en *vel'* ope (verb)	
e*pit*ome	Use four syllables — not "epi-tome."
escape	Use "s" — not "excape."
et cetera	Use "t" — not "ex cetera."
everlasting	Use "a" — not "everlusting."
ewe	Pronounce "you."
exalt vs. exult	
exercise vs. exorcise	
faithful vs. faith-filled	Pronounce all consonants carefully.
family	Use three syllables — not "famly."

February	Use "r" — not "Febooary" or "Febyouary."
figure	Not "figger"
fuel	Use two syllables — not "fule"
fulfillment	Use all "ls," especially *"ful"*
gifts	Use "fts"— not "giffs"
government	Use "r" and "n" — not "govenment" or "goverment"
grievous	Use two syllables — not "gree vi ous."
guard vs. God	
heifer	Pronounce "heffer."
heinous	Pronounce "haynus."

hewn	Pronounce "h you n" — not "hoon."
hostile	*"Hos' til"*
hospitable	Four syllables; it is easier if the accent is on "pit."
hue	Pronounce "h you."

immo*ral*'ity vs. immor*tal*'ity

***im*'pious**	Stress the first syllable; second syllable uses short vowel sound.
-ing	Use final "g."

in*iq*'uity vs. in*eq*'uity

***in*'sult (noun) vs. in*sult*' (verb)**

ir*rep*'arable	Use five syllables and do not pronounce as "irre*pair*able."

ir*rev*'ocable	Use five syllables and do not pronounce as "irre*vok*eable."
jewels	Use two syllables — not "jools."
jewelry	Not "jewlery"
Job	Not employment — not a job
Judaism	Use four syllables.
kindness	Pronounce "d" — not "kine ness."
laud vs. Lord	
law vs. lore	
length	The "g" is not silent.
lintel	Not "lentil"

listener	Use three syllables — not "lisner."
loins vs. lions	
Lord vs. lard	
lyre	Pronounce "liar."
mischievous	Use three syllables — not "mis chee' vi ous."
midst	Use "d" — not mist.
mouths	Use "th" — not mouse.
nuclear	Use three syllables — not "nukular."
oblation	Not "ovulation."
obvious	Pronounce the "b."
our	Use two syllables, like "hour."

particularly	Use five syllables.
persevere vs. preserve	
picture vs. pitcher	
poem	Use two syllables — not "pome."
poetry	Use three syllables.
poor vs. pore	
posterity vs. prosperity	
posthumous	Not "post humorous"
*pref***erable**	Not pre*fer*able
princes vs. princess	
prize vs. price	
*proc'***urator**	Not "procur'ator."

prophecy (noun) vs.
prophesy (verb)   Profesee vs. profesigh

prophesying   Not "prophesizing"

proscribed vs. prescribed

prostrate vs. prostate

recognize   Use "g" — not "reconize."

*ref'*use **(noun) vs. re***fuse'* **(verb)**

*res'*pite   Not "re*spite*"

reverence vs. reference For "v" (voiced), set teeth
                            into the bottom lip.
                            For "f" (voiceless), place
                            teeth *behind* the lower lip.

ruin   Use two syllables —
                            not "rune."

saw vs. sore

schism	"Skiz-m"
scourge	"Skurge" — not "skoorge" or "skorge."
sheaves	Use "v" — not sheeps.
so' **journ**	"*So'*-jern
statute vs. statue	
subliminally	Use five syllables.
suite vs. suit	
sword	Do not pronounce the "w"
synod	"*Sin'*-od"
temperature	Use four syllables.
tempest vs. temptress	
told vs. toll	
una*nim'*ity	Use five syllables.

unfathomable	Use five syllables.
vineyard	"Vinyard," not "vine yard"
violent	Use three syllables — not "vylent."
width	Use "d" and "th"
with	Clearly enunciate "th" with tongue between the teeth.
woman vs. women	
Zion	Use two syllables — not "zine."

In Conclusion

If you do not read the entire paragraph, you may consider me a heretic. So please stay with me on this! I am sorry, but I do not believe "The Lord God has given me a well-trained tongue." Taken out of context, I do not believe that quotation from the Book of the Prophet Isaiah, which we read every Palm Sunday of the Lord's Passion.

Indeed, the Lord God gave each of us a tongue, but we ourselves must work to develop it into becoming "well-trained." This gift from the Lord is unique to each of us, but the ability to use it properly should be our gift to God in appreciation. How well we use it depends on how we apply ourselves. What better reason have we to improve than to proclaim his word more effectively?

Vocal Health

A healthy voice is the product of a healthy body and mind. A voice reacts to all changes in physical and emotional states. Yes, even atmospheric differences. Therefore, to keep the voice healthy, we must keep ourselves healthy.

When we purchase an expensive item, we care for it and treat it kindly. We spend a great deal of money for these precious objects and we guard them carefully. But the voice within each of us came "without paying and without cost" (Isaiah) and we sometimes treat it with abandon and take it for granted.

Tone produced in a relaxed throat and fully supported by the breath travels farther and more pleasantly than that emanating from a tense mechanism. Screaming or yelling, especially at times of peak emotion such as anger or fear, is particularly detrimental because the throat, along with the entire body, becomes extremely tense. Not only is the sound hard on the individual, but its harshness is also hard on the ears of the listeners.

Taking care of your voice includes not screaming at sports events or rock concerts. Avoid yelling as you react to any happening. I realize it takes great self-control not to jump up and down and cheer loudly when your favorite team is winning. Realize how dearly you will pay for this abuse to your voice and for how many days it will not be normal, but unpleasantly hoarse.

I dread parties with loud music and being forced to talk over the din; I try to reserve conversation for the lull in the music and by using correct technique, avoid problems. Conversations on planes or subways, whenever there is heavy background noise, even cars with loud stereos, all these are potentially bad on a voice and should be situations for concern especially if the voice is to be used publicly in a short time.

A little restraint is so much wiser than spending time regretting your lack of wisdom in the use — or more correctly, the abuse — of your instrument. We would not expose a precious violin to the elements or wear an expensive ring while using a harsh cleanser. In other words, we exert care for these man-made possessions and rightfully so. Yet so often, we fail to be considerate in the care and use of a priceless gift of God — a voice!

The vocal mechanism is not overly delicate. A voice that is the product of good technique can withstand extensive use. A tired or strained voice loses quality and becomes dry and uninteresting in quality. Voices used by tired or indisposed individuals are strained because the body is straining to perform. Tiredness, even depression, tends to cut the range as well as the quality of the speaking voice and allows the tone to become monotonous and dull.

Speak at a pitch level comfortable for you — allowing room for pitches to rise or drop as desired. Do not force the voice higher or lower than its optimum level.

Laryngitis? Stop using your voice! Probably one of the most painful things any of us must endure is silence and not speaking. Do not even *try* to sing over any form of laryngitis, and keep speaking to a minimum. Whispering can cause even more strain than using the voice in its normal fashion.

Sometimes the pharynx and tonsil area can be sore but, despite the pain, use is not damaging to the voice. However, if the problem is in the larynx itself, there may be no soreness or difficulty in swallowing, only the telltale hesitation prior to phonation. This is when silence is the best treatment. The cords are swollen and inflamed and speaking, or even attempting to do so, will only exacerbate the situation and prolong the recovery process.

Many people feel hot tea with honey or lemon is helpful. Actually, avoid very hot or very cold liquids. Whatever you do to soothe the upper area of the throat (pharynx) does not touch the larynx itself; no lozenges, cough drops or anything you swallow has any curative effect on the vocal cords themselves; these remedies only alleviate the soreness in the upper throat. The best remedy is a good book — in other words, silence!

Inhaling steam is often recommended. This does not mean putting your head close to a steaming kettle; such action can be disastrous to the entire nasal and pharyngeal areas. Instead, simply sit in your kitchen and while the kettle boils, read a good book

— you might even study a passage from an upcoming assignment. A humidifier is a more sophisticated replacement for your kettle.

How often in summer do you awaken with a strange dryness and a vague hoarseness, feeling your voice has dropped at least a third in pitch? Prolonged use of air conditioning can create this unnatural dryness in the nose and throat areas as it does its job, not only cooling the air but dehumidifying it. Those of us who live in low-lying areas near coastlines are accustomed to a higher level of humidity, and when it is removed from the air we breathe we sense an uncomfortable dryness. This is noticed especially upon awakening after a night's sleep in an air-conditioned room. The nose and pharyngeal areas, as well as the larynx itself, have a feeling of discomfort and the voice displays a strange quality of hoarseness. A tall glass of water will not alleviate this soreness, but the steam of a prolonged shower will be more helpful. While the acute dryness in the larynx is untouched by anything you swallow, just normal breathing in a steamy shower situation will tend to be of value.

A post-nasal drip can be very annoying and there is a strong inclination to constantly clear the voice by coughing. A chronic condition that recurs should receive medical attention. However, most people react to different irritants on a short-term basis. One very big offender for those involved in a church situation is incense.

Many times, the urge to cough, or clear the voice — "speaker's cough," as it is often called — is psychological and a nervous habit. It is something that must be worked at mentally and controlled; it is not only annoying to listeners but counter-productive.

Rather than give in to the urge to keep clearing your throat by coughing, swallow. I am well aware that swallowing involves the esophagus and the vocal cords are encased in the trachea, but the two passageways are so closely placed that the action of swallowing creates enough movement that it tends to dislodge annoying bits of phlegm. (It also has a psychological value.) Think for a moment. If you bump into a table with objects on it but do not touch the objects themselves, they still move because of their contact with the table. So it is with the throat.

Avoid phlegm-producing foods, especially just prior to any public speaking or singing. Milk, cheese, in fact, any dairy products, soda, sweets of all sorts, particularly chocolate, are prime offenders.

People who use their voices wisely and correctly are not the victims of nodes. These little nodules that form on the vocal folds are the result of gross misuse of either the singing or speaking voice. Even after surgical removal, they can recur if the method of using the vocal mechanism is not changed, guided by a knowledgeable therapist or teacher. An injured athlete returns slowly to a sport; likewise, returning to full use of the voice must be directed and gradual. Remember, whether it is due to laryngitis or nodes, any dysfunction of the voice is best treated by vocal rest; avoid even whispering.

One of life's most precious gifts is common sense and a determination to put it into practice. Use it to find a good balance between hypochondria and reck-lessness. Dress appropriately for the weather, get sufficient rest and avoid conditions that would make you more prone to illness. Wisdom in its use and understanding its mechanism can prevent problems and preserve the longevity of the voice.

Quintilian, the Roman author who died in 59 A.D., wrote the first work on public speaking, "On Oratory As an Art." In it he tells his readers to "lead a simple life, eat sensibly, get plenty of rest and sleep." Through all the centuries and with all that modern medical science has to offer, no suggestion can be any wiser or more valid than this. Since a voice is encased in a body, the condition of that body has a direct bearing on the condition of the voice. So Quintilian cannot be disputed: take care of yourself and you will be taking care of your voice.

PART THREE: NATIONAL SURVEY RESULTS AND RESPONSES

When I first began this book, I conducted two surveys (April 1997). One was directed to the liturgical commissions and offices of worship in all archdioceses and many dioceses throughout the country. Seventy-five forms were mailed and seventy were returned. The second survey went to parishes of varying economic and ethnic backgrounds in all parts of the United States. Seventy-five were mailed and sixty-eight were returned.

In order to update the figures, another questionnaire was mailed to parishes on a nationwide scale in 1999. Eighty-eight of the one hundred surveys mailed were returned in time for this book. Participants were selected to include a variety of locations and situations:

- metropolitan, suburban and rural areas

- large communities (with schools, convents, etc.) and small parishes

- rectories with several priests and those with only one

Names were chosen with care and purpose. Although the questions were posed in a checklist format, many respondents added interesting thoughts at the conclusion of the questions. None of the surveys was intended as a scientific study but rather an informal overview of the training of lectors in order to provide me with necessary information for this book.

The most recent survey, its responses and pertinent comments appear on the following pages.

Survey and Results

1. How many Masses do you have on Sunday?
While this question has nothing to do with lectors themselves, it sheds light on the proportion of lectors to scheduled Masses.

2. How many lectors do you have in your parish?
Naturally, there is a great variety; some parishes have a bare minimum of lectors but surprisingly,

most have quite a few. There is definitely an increase in the number of readers in this latest inquiry.

What I found particularly interesting were the comments written at the conclusion of the questionnaires by the pastor or director of liturgy.

One moderator added the thought, "We have way too many lectors, but I don't know what to do about it." I cannot imagine a parish having too many *effective* lectors. It might be that the selection process is not selective enough in choosing only those with a genuine ability to proclaim and communicate the word.

Another offered: "I have many lectors who are inadequate but I feel reluctant to drop them." Maybe some of these people should have been directed to other ministries in the first place. I did receive one response indicating the new moderator had "inherited" a situation such as this and was trying to weed out the ineffective. With great tact, the director might find a way to guide these lectors to a different phase of liturgy. The word of the Lord deserves special consideration.

I can understand the desire to involve as many people as possible. However, no skill is developed if there are so many readers on the roster that they read very infrequently. Each assignment feels like the first one and starting all over again. No sense of the role of lector is acquired or felt. A fair amount of frequency in reading is mandatory if a good proclaimer is to be developed.

Another way to utilize a large roster of lectors is to assign two lectors per Mass. In fact, if there is no deacon, a third lector can be assigned: one for each reading and a third for the Prayer of the Faithful. Some parishes use this programming very successfully. Rather than lectoring infrequently, it is preferable to do just one reading per Mass.

Some of the awkward aspects of the selection process might be alleviated if a person with expertise from outside the parish is called in to evaluate or audition lectors. This relieves the parish priests of the rather unpleasant situation involved in choosing and eliminating. The outside person, being just that, an outsider, can judge solely on ability to proclaim, completely unaware of the individual's status in the parish. Lectoring should never be a "reward."

Some parishes restrict people to one ministry only, which allows opportunities for more parishioners to become involved in the liturgy. This seems prudent on the part of the clergy and fair to the parish. Often we see the same faces in all aspects of parish activities, whether liturgical or social. This frequently prevents other people from coming forth to volunteer their services because it seems to them to be a "closed corporation," not to be penetrated. The thought of "one ministry only" can be a way to lessen the problem of too many lectors, since some applicants could be directed to a different form of service. Personally, I would prefer a parish to have fewer lectors who were trained and well-prepared to proclaim the text with conviction, rather than a larger roster who lack a true sense of this ministry.

To allow a lector to develop all the qualifications needed, assignments need to be at intervals of three or four weeks. Less frequently than this, it just does not happen.

3. Does the parish provide any training for them?

Almost all parishes responded "Yes" to this, but there is no way of knowing how extensive the training is and what form the training takes.

4. Is time spent on

      a) Vocal development?
      b) Breathing?
      c) Dynamics of speech?
      d) Delivery of the text?
      e) Demeanor of the lector?

In most parishes surveyed, the training given is meager at best. Though many responded "Yes" to Question 3 regarding in-parish work, the answers to Question 4 and the breakdown of the form of training were strange. All but four percent checked "No" to breathing, though they answered positively to the various types of technique suggested. Truly, the understanding of correct breathing is at the root of all vocal training, whether speech or song. Without explanation and direction in the proper use of the breath there can be no vocal development. Thus, there is no equipment to allow dynamics of speech and, consequently, the effective delivery of the text.

It was interesting to note that only two parishes of those surveyed have professional people working with and coaching lectors on a regular basis; they are both volunteers. Even more interesting (and I would say, logical) is the location of these two parishes. At opposite ends of the country, one is in the Archdiocese of Los Angeles and the other in the Diocese of Brooklyn — areas adjacent to the meccas of the film and theater worlds. The explanation may be that there is a high concentration of people equipped to do this type of work in these dioceses. It does not seem to be a coincidence.

5. Is an exegesis or scriptural commentary given by a priest or deacon?

This was answered overwhelmingly in the negative. Only 20 percent offered any exegesis to the lectors.

I fully comprehend how overworked the deacons and priests are. It is shocking to check parishes throughout the country and realize how many have only one priest. In some areas, there is only a lay administrator while a priest works on a circuit, covering several parishes. This is truly frightening and definitely should be the proverbial wake-up call for the laity.

However, I still wish there could be the opportunity for someone knowledgeable to offer an exegesis. At the very least a biblical commentary could be placed at the disposal of lectors, and its use strongly suggested.

With the appearance of the new lectionary, some publishers of the paperback books used by the congregation are now including a short exegesis of the readings for each Sunday and holy day liturgy. Though this may be minimal, it is a help and all lectors should be made aware of these explanations and urged to study them carefully.

If there is no such pamphlet-type item available in the pews, the moderator might be able to suggest a local Catholic bookstore where one of these inexpensive publications or a biblical commentary can be ordered and purchased.

6. Do you have a dress code?

To the question regarding dress code, one pastor wrote, "No, but it sounds like a good idea!"

Half the respondents have a dress code. My strong feeling is that this is contingent on the selection and training of lectors. If lectors are chosen carefully and instructed in the demeanor appropriate for this ministry, proper dress will be automatic.

I was once told of an executive at a local bank who, on business days, was always dressed properly in a suit and tie. However, when he walked to the ambo to read on Sundays he looked as if he had just come in from plowing the fields. There is a line between casual and sloppy! It would seem prudent to have a robe or alb in the sacristy in the event of an emergency, a substitution or if a lector deemed inappropriately dressed is to proclaim the word.

7. Are all applicants welcomed to this ministry? Many are called, but are few chosen?

Most parishes, responding positively, qualified by adding, "If they are capable." "Welcome, yes — installed, no." "I hope not, but probably!" And so on. Interestingly, a few added, "Yes, unless in an invalid marriage."

8. How are lectors selected?
Volunteer?
Chosen by clergy?

Sixty-five percent checked both "Volunteer" and "Chosen by clergy." The remainder were volunteers.

9. Is there a specific qualification process (e.g., auditions)?

In 65 percent of the responding parishes, some form of selection process is carried on; there is no way of knowing how extensive it is. The moderator (or whoever will train and assign prospective lectors) should audition people.

Sending out a call for new readers, a priest friend put an article in the parish bulletin which read, "Those wishing to be considered for acceptance to the ministry of lector . . ." The important word here is *considered.* This discreetly implies that all who come will not automatically become readers. "Audition" is a scary and intimidating word. It might be a wise idea to avoid its use. Instead, phrase it the way my friend did. But all lectors must be heard (and please God, trained!) before their names are added to the roster. This avoids numerous problems.

It is not fair to ask the aspirants to do a "cold reading," that is, to hand them a selection and ask them to proclaim it without time to prepare. Choose a passage beforehand; let the auditioner study it for a few minutes, then let the person try it. If there are several people to be heard, a different passage should be given to each; otherwise, it is unfair to the first person. After a few have read it, the selection becomes familiar and the last people to read have a much easier task.

The moderator must listen for clarity of voice and quality, possible speech problems, body language and attitude, and the potential for development. There should also be a sense of willingness to cooperate and improve. It is also necessary to get a sense of the spirituality of the person.

The motivation for being a lector should be questioned. I've heard people say, "I love to perform!" A lector is not a performer! A lector is the instrument through which God's word comes to life, and spirituality is necessary. Perhaps we should say the *potential* is necessary. There should be at least a glimmer of that in the aspirant. Surely, it will, it *must* develop as one delves more deeply into the scriptures. Lectoring must not be an opportunity for a person to "perform."

I truly feel a great responsibility is placed on those who select lectors. In any interview situation, it is not unusual to be asked, "Why do you want this position and what do you hope to bring to it?" It is reasonable to ask this of the applicants.

The moderator should be able to pick up "vibes" or body language from the individual. The whole bearing of a person gives off a sense of amiability or a sense of arrogance, one of extreme self-confidence or a lack of it; the attitude conveys so much and it is necessary to evaluate it in the selection process. Once again, the body language speaks loudly.

In listening to someone read, the moderator must not focus too strongly on pacing or volume because the person is largely unfamiliar with the acoustical situation of the church. Also, if the aspiring lector has had little or no experience in public speaking, he or she will be almost conversational in pacing or volume. This is all "fixable." A speech impediment is not. Many of these can be improved but need a speech therapist and cannot be addressed or corrected in a regular program for readers.

Someone once told me her psychiatrist thought being a lector would be good therapy for her. Both the pastor and the moderator agreed that this would be a misuse of the ministry — that it would indeed be an abuse!

The feeling of an aspirant should be, "What can be given? What can be contributed by lectoring?" But believe me, no one ever gives a fraction to this ministry compared to what it gives the lector in return. We could paraphrase the words from President Kennedy's inaugural address: "Ask not what lectoring can do for you. Ask what you can do for lectoring!"

10. Do you have an age requirement? If so, what is the minimum age?

Three years ago when the first survey was taken, the minimum age in most parishes surveyed (where a minimum age existed) was eighteen and "fully initiated," that is, confirmed.

This recent survey indicated there are more confirmed teenagers reading: "sixteen or high school juniors." Few parishes answered simply "high school," which would suggest fourteen and over. I can comprehend the desire to involve teens but I sincerely feel that in most cases younger teens are still at an unsettled time with their voices and are not really capable of carrying the weight of the scripture. If someone works with them, not only technically, but also on the exegesis, then it is more plausible. Even then, many young teenagers lack the stamina for lengthy passages, such as Easter Vigil or Passion readings. They start strong, but after a time become tired and all sorts of problems surface.

Children are frequent ministers of the word at school or other liturgies with children. This practice was apparent nationwide.

It always surprises me that children are permitted to be lectors but almost never are cantors. From my own personal experience, I sang professionally before school age, but I would have been overwhelmed at the thought of being a lector — even as a teenager. The text would have frightened me. In my years of experience as a teacher, I have worked with both music and scripture. I can assure you it is infinitely easier to teach someone to sing a song or a hymn than to proclaim the word.

Anyone singing has the support of the accompaniment; a singer, though a soloist, is not completely alone. If a younger cantor is not as secure as would be desired, the organist can gently feed and direct through the playing. That is precisely the idea; there is *support* and there can be reliance on a good organist, which overcomes the feeling the lector has of being completely alone. Young singers have instrumentalists to prevent them from running away with the tempo, but young lectors have no accompanists to keep their pace from accelerating.

The music itself gives a strong indication of the flavor and mood of the hymn and suggests the underlying message the lyric contains; the readings have only the words themselves. It is mandatory that young lectors (and some not-so-young lectors) are given help with the meaning in order to convey the proper message of the text.

11. Does your diocese provide any workshops for lectors?

If so, do your readers avail themselves of this opportunity?

To say the United States is a vast country is an understatement. Some areas are sparsely populated and the diocese is very widespread. Naturally, in places such as these, a diocesan training program is not feasible; an in-parish preparation is conducted in some localities, sometimes by the parish itself and sometimes by people sent from the Liturgical Commission of the diocese.

More than 80 percent of the responding archdioceses and dioceses offer a training program; of these, five percent of diocesan offices send a team into rural parishes. Unfortunately, 25 percent of parishes do not use these opportunities, or if the parish does, the individual lectors do not.

12. Are you using the new lectionary?

A hundred percent answered in the affirmative.

13. Do you find the format, pagination and translation improved and more beneficial for readers?

All agreed that the pagination and format improved. Not only is it easier on the eye, but the sense-lines make it much more beneficial for lectors. Wider spacing creates a less congested appearance. It also helps to prevent the hazard of losing one's place. (I cannot count the times novice lectors have told me they had nightmares about losing their place in the reading.) The new format is a welcome change and appreciated by all lectors.

14. Do you plan to revitalize your lector program in conjunction with the publication of the new lectionary?
Only 35 percent responded affirmatively to the idea of revitalizing their lector programs. Six percent replied, "Not at this time," indicating that it may be under consideration.

One pastor remarked, "The need to revitalize exists, regardless of the new translation." I do not know if he was referring to his own parish, or to lectors in general. In either case, I heartily agree.

I do feel the advent of the new lectionary has focused attention on what is too often an autonomous ministry. Anything that causes pastors and/or moderators to recognize the need to revitalize, restructure, or in any way further the technique and scriptural knowledge of their lectors is most welcome and certain to be appreciated by congregations. If there is little true comprehension of the words, then they are just that — words! I have said this so often: "If it doesn't make any sense to the reader, it cannot make sense to the listener!"

PART FOUR: TIDBITS FOR LECTORS

In many respects, writing a book such as this is not very different from the cleaning a house undergoes prior to a party or overnight guests. Regardless of how hard you work, there is always one more piece of silver to be polished, one more vase of flowers to be arranged. Any host or hostess can identify with this situation.

The following topics relate directly to lectors. They are small but important things I've picked up over many years from the ministry of reading and from the ministry of training lectors individually and in workshops. Some have been alluded to earlier but warrant further explanation.

Eucharistic Presence

I will ask your indulgence while I share with you an incident that touched me very deeply. God has been exceedingly good to me by bringing me into contact with many wonderful, loving people. Among these were my physician and his wife who treated me like a daughter, after God called my own parents to his heavenly kingdom. One evening, sitting in their kitchen over coffee, Lillian talked about a neighbor's funeral Mass she had attended that morning. She was impressed by the liturgy and felt that it should have been a source of consolation to all. Then she asked me to explain the Mass.

Lillian wanted to discuss Holy Communion. I tried not to over-explain things or get too technical but preferred to say it simply: "We believe this is Jesus." She must have grasped, however, the fuller impact of my statement. She hastened to tell me she did believe in Jesus, that he came into the world and made it a better place by preaching a message of love. She went on, "If we truly love one another as he taught, we would not hurt people."

Then she questioned why Catholics received Communion in different ways: some by extending their hands and others, their tongue. With an intensity that overwhelmed me, this Jewish lady said, "I would take Jesus in my hand and just want to clasp him close to my heart. I understand that in swallowing you are internalizing. [Remember, she was a physician's wife!] But I would just want to hold him so very close."

Tears rolled down my face with the tremendous impact of her sincerity. Then and there I just wished that more Catholics would be given the realization experienced by this woman who was of another faith.

I could not help but think of the CBS/*New York Times* survey regarding Catholics and their belief in the "Real Presence." Here was a Jewish woman with a powerful sense of what the reception of Holy Communion is truly about. How strongly she desired to clasp the eucharistic Jesus close to her heart! I hope that her example helps others accept, believe in and value this most blessed gift.

The people receiving Holy Communion at that funeral Mass had no idea of the example they were giving anybody or of the impact they had on Lillian. We can never really be aware of how our actions are being viewed and perceived by others.

Nerves

Remember, nerves are controlled by control! No, this is not a mistake or an error in printing, but a fact.

If you are in control of your instrument, be it a voice, a piano, an organ (or even a car) and are sure of your material, your security can help control your nerves.

Focus

During a reading, technique cannot be a matter of concern. It must be set beforehand with training and practice. When the time comes, technique must be secure so that concern is focused entirely on communicating the message to the listeners. If you lack control, you must go back to the drawing board and do the necessary homework until the technical skills are fully in place and implemented. Then, and only then, can you expect technique to work for you, when it is subconsciously and completely a part of you. You must always concentrate on *what* you are doing — not *how* you are doing it.

One at a Time

The lector is not a "jack-of-all-trades." It is permissible to be a lector, a leader of song and a eucharistic minister (if your parish sanctions multiple ministries) but not at the same Mass: *One ministry per Mass.* If you choose, however, you may attend successive Masses and serve in a different capacity at each, but not all at once. Should there be an emergency and the presiding celebrant requests a lector to also act as a special minister of the Eucharist, then by all means, comply with his request.

Dry Mouth

In an emergency situation, if your mouth is completely dry, irritate the tip of your tongue, either by gently nibbling on the tip of it or by rubbing it against the back of your lower teeth. This should stimulate the salivary glands and induce saliva to flow. True, it is not going to quench your thirst as would a glass of water but it will help to alleviate the extreme dryness when nothing else is available. While we are on the subject of thirst, do not drink water full of ice! Room temperature water is best; avoid ice water because the extreme cold constricts your throat.

Stand Still!

When standing for a prolonged period during the Mass, there is a tendency to rock back and forth. This can be avoided in a very easy manner; let the calves of your legs touch the chair or bench where you would be seated. Making contact with a solid object gives a sense of stability and prevents wobbling, which can be distracting to anyone watching. Some people have a natural propensity for constantly moving, shifting their weight from the left foot to the right, or rocking forward on their toes and back into their heels. As Mass begins, making contact with the chair will create a calming stability that steadies your body and evinces poise.

Remember that your feet must be firmly planted on the ground without swaying as you deliver the scriptures. Otherwise, your volume will be changing constantly. Standing erect and still is a discipline that does not come easily to some, but it is a necessary "ingredient in the plan."

And When Sitting —

Please, please, please, keep your knees together and your feet on the floor! Sit up straight. Remember, you are not at home in your favorite chair watching TV. A relaxed body is not a collapsed body. If your legs are very short, sit forward on the chair with your feet on the floor.

Do Not Play Editor!

Do not delete, embellish or in any way edit the text. Read it exactly as it appears. Under no circumstance should anyone ever knowingly and deliberately alter the scripture. The lectionary used in your church is the book you read (never read from the paperback in the pews); this is the exact text to be proclaimed. If a reader changes or omits any part of it, he or she is far exceeding the role of lector and is never empowered to make substitutions or deletions of any phrases.

Long Form vs. Short Form

If there is an option for a shorter version of a reading, always consult the celebrant before Mass as to his preference. Do not take for granted that the short form is to be used. Perhaps the celebrant at a particular Mass may have based part of his homily on the passages that are eliminated if the long form is not used. It is not only a courtesy to ask which form he prefers, but it also indicates to the priest that you have prepared and are aware of the two possibilities.

Hair Styles

Long flowing tresses have always been in style from biblical times to the present. However, loosely falling hair is an annoyance to readers and a distraction to listeners if it is falling in one's face, particularly the eyes. The lector then tends to keep shaking her head or playing with it to remove it from her face. Pins, clips or hair spray can be used to prevent this bothersome situation. Whatever the style, it must be one which does not encourage or necessitate a hand repeatedly brushing it back or in any way toying with locks that should have been locked in place beforehand!

Last-Minute Substitutes

If your parish frequently needs substitutes at the last moment and calls upon unassigned lectors attending Mass, it is wise to look at the readings before arriving at church.

Often those called from the congregation in an emergency are inappropriately dressed. A thoughtful gesture on the part of priests or other staff members of a parish in anticipation of just such a situation is to have a robe or alb in the sacristy ready for an unscheduled reader. This avoids the horror of seeing a lector in jeans, a tennis outfit or the like. Such attire distracts the congregation, embarrasses the individual and disrespects the liturgy.

Objects of Prepositions

I have a very strong aversion to hearing people (including priest celebrants) read passages in which the preposition is accentuated instead of its object. We never do it in ordinary speech; why we allow it to creep into the readings is beyond my comprehension. It is disappointing to hear so may deacons, priests and bishops giving a poor example on this point. Many lectors admire and emulate the priests and subconsciously copy their inflectional patterns.

Even with repetitious phrases the emphasis should be placed on the object; for example, "We pray to the *Lord.*" We do not pray *at* the Lord, *around* the Lord or *under* the Lord. There is no reason to accentuate anything but the object, "Lord," in this case.

Set the Tone

If a television program does not engage your enthusiasm at the outset, you reach for the remote. When you read a book — if it starts slowly and does not interest you immediately — you put it aside.

Actually, the lector sets the tone for the Mass. If the proclamation is not well delivered, the assembly settles back and turns its attention off. Once turned off, people do not readily turn on again the minute the celebrant continues with the Gospel and his homily. The priest almost has to shoot off rockets or balloons to win back their concentration. We can easily say that the responsibility placed on lectors is genuine; they can take the congregation along with them or lose them, thanks to their delivery.

Proper Reverences

In the "old days," that is, before the Second Vatican Council, the priest entered the sanctuary carrying his chalice. He bowed to the tabernacle while holding his chalice and paten before ascending the altar steps and placing these on the altar.

Today, the chalice and other vessels are placed on a credence table near the altar, and the lectionary is placed "at the lectern" (GIRM, 80b). The lectionary is not carried in the entrance procession. The deacon or, in his absence, a reader carries the *Book of the Gospels* in the entrance procession (Introduction to the *Book of the Gospels,* 9; GIRM, 82). When carrying the *Book of the Gospels* in the procession, the reader "walks in front of the priest; otherwise he [or she] walks with the other ministers. Upon reaching the altar, the reader makes the proper reverence along with the priest, goes up to the altar and places the *Book of the Gospels* on it. Then he [or she] takes his [or her] place in the sanctuary with the other ministers" (GIRM, 148–49). Elsewhere we learn that for the reader at this point the "proper reverence . . . is a low bow or, if there is a tabernacle containing the blessed sacrament, a genuflection" (GIRM, 84).

If there is a tabernacle with the blessed sacrament in the altar area, the priest celebrant and other ministers genuflect toward it only in the processions at the beginning and end, but never during the celebration of the Mass itself. Cross and candle bearers bow their heads instead of genuflecting at those times. If the tabernacle is elsewhere, however, the ministers bow toward the altar. A bow is a sign of reverence or honor given to persons or representations of those persons. There are two kinds: a) an inclination of the head at the name of the three Divine Persons, Jesus, the Blessed Virgin Mary or of the saint in whose honor the celebration takes place; b) a profound inclination of the body toward the altar if there is no tabernacle (see GIRM 2000, 275).

Monotony

A monotonous delivery is different from a monotone. A monotone is exactly what the term implies: a voice that employs one pitch, not varying higher or lower. A speaker can use a large variance in pitch, a somewhat interesting inflectional pattern and even differences in rhythm, but if these changes are repetitive, the delivery can be considered monotonous due to the constancy of the sound. A pitch or rhythmic pattern that is constantly reiterated can be as boring as speech totally devoid of inflection. This is an especially common problem in the reading of the psalms, making it mandatory to spend adequate time in their preparation.

Get up early!

Get up early enough to wake up your voice. Even more to the point, get up early enough to have breakfast. A glass of water does not do much to clear away all the "junk" which accumulates in the back of your throat during sleep. Singers or speakers will do much better if they have even a little toast; anything solid is more effective than fluid in ridding the overnight matter that settles in the back of the throat.

This is particularly important if you live alone and do not engage in any conversation before leaving for church. Do not inflict a sleepy, froggy voice on the congregation.

Finding the Reading

Many times, lectors arrive for Mass and, finding the lectionary closed and the marker askew, they are at a loss to find the readings for the day. Where do they turn if there is no clergy or knowledgeable person on the scene?

First, in each sacristy there is an "ordo," a little book that, in addition to a necrology, lists all readings and other details of the Mass to be offered and saint to be honored each day. Refer to it, if only to confirm the correct choices for the day.

Many leaflet missals also have, at the beginning of each Mass listing, a small italicized number in parenthesis. For example:

On Sunday:
Fifth Sunday of Easter *(52)*

On a weekday:
Fifth Week of Easter *(287)*

Or on a Feast of Saints:
June 29
Solemnity of Sts. Peter and Paul *(591)*

These numbers in parentheses refer to the number of the reading or set of readings, *not* the page number in the lectionary. Therefore, they are universal and the same in all editions of the new lectionary. These numbers are found on the inside of the pages, near the binding, as opposed to the placement of regular page numbers.

Semicolons vs. Commas

Semicolons separate complete, independent clauses. Hence, a semicolon is treated inflectionally like a period; the voice drops in pitch as it does at the conclusion of a sentence. A comma used to separate words in a series or unfinished thoughts demands that the voice suggest there is more to follow. The clause is incomplete, and consequently the voice must convey that incompletion. Therefore, the pitch should remain up to keep the thought-line vital and imply suspension.

Final Comment

An Academy Award winner being interviewed was asked, "What is your secret? What made you successful?"

Without hesitation his reply came: "Being prepared and studying constantly."

Need I add more?

POSTLUDE

Only the Beginning

When a singer makes a Metropolitan Opera debut, when a young doctor receives an M.D. or when a young man is ordained a priest, it would seem each has attained his goal and has arrived at Parnassus. Despite the tremendous amount of study and sacrifice involved in achieving this level in life, in reality this is just the beginning. There is never an end to what can be learned to make a finer singer, a more astute doctor, or a more spiritual priest.

Why do so many lectors feel that after the first time at the ambo they have all the technique and insight they need? Even many of those who assign them leave them to their own devices and spend no further time or effort in attempting to improve their skills and increase their understanding of the scriptures.

The young singer, regardless of how great the response from the press, realizes it takes even more study and striving to maintain the success. It is *only the beginning.*

The young physician, even if he or she becomes a noted brain surgeon, knows there must be constant study to learn new, and ever newer, techniques. Receiving the doctor status is *only the beginning.*

The young priest realizes soon after ordination what he knew years before when he first responded to the call; his life will be one of constant study and searching to enable him to become a more deeply spiritual priest. Ordination is indeed *only the beginning.*

There is a continuing need to better ourselves as lectors — the voice itself, its use and the technique of proclamation, a deeper understanding of the Scriptures to allow a more knowledgeable delivery of the message to congregation members. If a day comes when you feel you have achieved all that is possible, and it is just routine, resign.

Vladimir Horowitz, to his dying day, recognized the need for constant work at the keyboard, if not to learn new material, to refresh and polish compositions he had performed for a whole lifetime. Beverly Sills had a lesson every day of her performing life.

These people realized the responsibility they had to maintain what they had achieved and constantly sought to keep scores and scripts vibrant and alive.

There is no perfection in this world, but we must constantly strive to attain it. What better reason is there than for the proclamation of the word? Always remember that if you are well prepared the delivery will be effective.

To all of you, those aspiring to be lectors, those who are novice lectors and lectors of much experience: I wish you the joy and awesome sense of spiritual enrichment that comes from probing into the meanings of the scriptures and bringing them to life for the people of God, using your unique gift of God, your voice!

ACKNOWLEDGMENTS

Deo Gratias!

At the completion of any task, we usually say, "Thank God that's finished!" The intensity of the remark reacts to the immensity of what has just been completed.

This book has been in my heart and mind for many years, and I can truthfully say it has been an overwhelming venture. So, I do not say in a light-hearted manner, "Thank God."

I do thank God every day of my life for all his goodness to me, for all he has given me. At the outset, he gave me the most incredible parents, whose lives were the exemplification of the Corporal Works of Mercy. Their generosity in sacrificing to educate and develop my God-given abilities knew no limits.

Again I say, *"Deo gratias!"*

In complex and often remote, circuitous ways, he brings various people to us who have a great impact on our lives. I often marvel at the way in which the

Master Designer weaves these individuals into the fabric of our lives!

Most Reverend Gerald M. Barbarito

Despite an extremely demanding schedule, Bishop Barbarito always took the time to inquire about the progress of this book, read sections of it, offered strong reinforcement and assured me of his spiritual support. I can never adequately voice my gratitude for his belief in this work and his willingness to endorse it.

Very Reverend Dennis M. Corrado, C.O.

Though God did not give me siblings, he has gifted me with some wonderful friends. One, in particular, is Father Corrado, who recognized my abilities and background and literally forced me to teach voice. I will always be grateful for his insistence, for his constant encouragement with this book, and of course, for his input in writing its foreword. I love you, dear friend, and always will!

Amelia Gagliano Chiera

My Ame! Her computer skills are surpassed only by her beautiful lyric soprano voice. I am most grateful for her time and technical assistance.

Reverend John P. Cush

When first I met him, Father Cush was but a few days ordained. However, he made a suggestion which was truly inspired and which channeled this book into the right hands. *Mille Grazie!*

Reverend John Gurrieri

Many years ago, I mentioned my intention to write a book for lectors to Father. Even then, he encouraged me to undertake the task. Now, at its completion, I am honored by his willingness to read the manuscript and his reaction to it as well.

Patricia Kossmann

In the ninety-year history of the Jesuit magazine, *America,* there had never been a layperson or a woman on the editorial staff. Ms. Kossmann has the distinction of being the first in both categories. I am delighted to have her support and endorsement.

Reverend James P. Moroney

"Indebtedness" is a gross understatement. I could never adequately express my gratitude to Father Moroney. His enthusiastic response and support were beyond measure — skyrocketing my spirits when the "going was tough." His offer to write the back cover of this book was an honor and joy I never dared to expect.

Marie Romano

This book would not have come about so easily without the patience and competence of another dear friend, Marie Romano. I treasure her friendship even more than her expertise. How many nights, after a full day of work, she began again at home and "burned the midnight oil" to type the manuscript. Marie is always gracious, always willing and always wearing her beautiful smile.

Reverend Monsignor Robert E. Welsh

An additional note of appreciation to my dear friend who not only began my involvement in this ministry but was kind in reading various stages of this manuscript and supportive enough to keep this writing going.

So many have been supportive and helpful in so many varied ways — some spiritually, some with constant encouragement, some with giving of their time and talent. These are just a few of the people who more than merit recognition and my sincere gratitude. Unintentionally, some will be omitted; I ask their pardon.

Eleanora Abruzzese

Monsignor Thomas F. Brady

Marissa Cavanagh

Reverend James K. Cunningham

Laura Incampo

Sister Bernadette Izzo, O.P.

Jim Mara

Reverend John G. McLoughlin

Monsignor Anthony F. Sherman

Reverend Timothy J. Teahan

Reverend Gerard T. Walker

and all those who responded to my survey

As I began this book with a quotation from Oscar Hammerstein, so I shall end it. In *The King and I,* Anna sings:

It's a very ancient saying
But a true and honest thought,
That if you become a teacher
By your pupils you'll be taught.

To all the lectors I have taught through all the years, whether individually or in groups, my heartfelt thanks. Each of you taught me something that contributed to this book. May you always cherish the opportunity and privilege of being the instrument that brings God's word to life!

Mary Lyons
May 5, 2000

P.S. It's raining! It's my kind of day, *Deo gratias!*